How to Develop Partnerships with Parents

This definitive resource provides a comprehensive range of activities and materials enabling you to equip your staff with the knowledge, confidence and skills they need to collaborate effectively with parents as part of their early years practice.

Packed with practical, reflective and team-based activities and templates, *How to Develop Partnerships with Parents* offers evidence-based information on working successfully with parents, and provides a range of materials to meet the specific training and development needs of your staff. Chapters emphasise the benefits of working closely with families, and acknowledge the particular needs of parents with children at various stages of development, and with SEND. Information and activities are presented in a unique, accessible format, meaning you can quickly access the materials most relevant for your staff and setting, to provide effective training and ensure that staff members can build outstanding working relationships with parents, collaborating with families to the benefit of the child.

With downloadable resources, activities and opportunities for reflection throughout, this will be essential reading for early years managers, students and practitioners, trainers and co-ordinators.

Teresa Wilson is Programme Director of the BA in Education Studies and until recently Programme Director of the Foundation Degree in Children's Development and Learning at the University of Reading, UK.

How to Develop Partnerships with Parents

A Practical Guide for the Early Years

Teresa Wilson

Routledge
Taylor & Francis Group

LONDON AND NEW YORK

First published 2019
by Routledge
2 Park Square, Milton Park, Abingdon, Oxon OX14 4RN

and by Routledge
711 Third Avenue, New York, NY 10017

Routledge is an imprint of the Taylor & Francis Group, an informa business

British Library Cataloguing-in-Publication Data
A catalogue record for this book is available from the British Library

Library of Congress Cataloging-in-Publication Data
Names: Wilson, Teresa, author.
Title: How to develop partnerships with parents : a practical guide for the early years / Teresa Wilson.
Description: Abingdon, Oxon ; New York, NY : Routledge, 2019. |
Includes bibliographic references and index.
Identifiers: LCCN 2018025583| ISBN 9781138220638 (hbk.) | ISBN 9781138220645 (pbk.) | ISBN 9781315412412 (ebk.)
Subjects: LCSH: Early childhood education—Parent participation. |
Education, Preschool—Parent participation.
Classification: LCC LB1139.35.P37 W55 2019 | DDC 372.21—dc23
LC record available at https://lccn.loc.gov/2018025583

ISBN: 9781138220638 (hbk)
ISBN: 9781138220645 (pbk)
ISBN: 9781315412412 (ebk)

Typeset in Sabon
by Florence Production Limited, Stoodleigh, Devon, UK

Visit the eResources: www.routledge.com/9781138220645

*To my mum, with love and thanks
for everything*

Contents

Acknowledgements

Thanks to all practitioners from First Steps Day Nursery who contributed to this book by letting me test some of the activities during their staff meetings in 2017. It was so helpful to listen to their discussions, comments and ideas. In particular, thank you to Christine Mountford, previous Nursery Manager and Sharon Scott, Deputy Manager.

Thanks to BabyCenter, L.L.C., for giving permission to include a message published on their website (p. 99).

Thanks also to all the people that I have worked with, in training or education (or both) whose training ideas would have influenced my development and therefore the creation of this material.

Finally, thank you for the editorial support I have received from Annamarie Kino and Elsbeth Wright.

Of course, all errors or omissions are mine alone.

1 | Making partnership with parents an outstanding quality in your setting

TABLE 1.1 Links to early years (EY) documentation

Teachers' Standards (Early Years), (NCTL, 2013)	Early years inspection handbook (Ofsted, updated 2018)	*Statutory framework for early years foundation stage (DfE, 2017)*
8.1 8.2 8.5 8.6	s. 150 (p. 31)	s. 3.20 (p. 21)

Working with parents is a fundamental part of early years practice, yet many practitioners have had little or no training in this part of their work, mainly because of the current limitations on funding from local authorities and the shortage of training time available in settings. However, research suggests that the quality of the relationship that takes place in pre-school settings can build bridges between families and professionals that confers longer-term benefits for all involved (Pirchio *et al.*, 2013). On a basic level, the relationship between a parent and practitioner can result in effective information sharing between all parties, leading to a greater understanding and a fuller picture of a child's experiences, likes, developmental information and disposition. Given that all planning should begin from knowledge of the individual child (Department for Education (DfE), 2017), the more complete the picture, the greater the opportunity for practitioners to be able to support that child's learning effectively.

This book provides practical and evidence-based guidance to best practice in working with parents that will help practitioners and early childhood students to work effectively with parents through developing a greater understanding of ways to build trusting relationships. It will also explain the purposes of partnership work. The activities are categorised by the length of time they might take (although this is always a variable according to other factors) and by the type:

longer activities,   short activities,

case studies,   overnight reflections.

They are suitable for all levels of practitioner.

This is a book that you can dip into, photocopy, pin on the wall, use for staff training, use for reflection, hold short training activities or mix and match for a staff training day, depending on the training/development needs. There are opportunities to complete activities and reflect upon particular areas or all areas and most importantly, you do not have to do it all at once. You can review your development at the end of each chapter.

Aims and structure of this practical guide

Aims of this toolkit

- to develop skills of practitioners in early years settings;
- to increase the confidence of practitioners and parents to work together in a spirit of mutual trust;
- to enable settings to review practice and offer support to their staff;
- to provide settings with templates which are compliant with current sector expectations in order to evidence practice.

Structure of this guide

The structure of the book leads practitioners through a process:

- Introduction to a topic with opportunities to assess current practice.
- Provision of training activities – enabling practitioners to reflect and build on their practice.
- Development of strategies for working with parents.
- Review of strengths and areas for development within the setting.

Activities are designed to reflect the time restraints in settings, and there will be a range of training sessions throughout the book that take different periods; for example, there will be:

overnight reflections that will help practitioners to prepare for a training session or a workshop. You can use discussions based on these as a starting exercise to a training session;

case studies – to use for training – either as part of a workshop or as individual exercises to discuss a topic area in more depth;

short activity (15 minutes) – quick, lively activities to generate ideas and discussion. Can be used as introductions to a session or standalone;

longer activity (45–60 minutes) – these exercises give practitioners more time to get to grips with a topic – this will allow debate and exploration, but time to identify strengths and strategies for development;

● quotes for reflection or discussion – marked in italicised font throughout.

You can use a selection of the activities to create a workshop – you can mix and match to suit your needs.

Please note that the timings are only rough guides and you can adapt many activities to make them fit into your own time structures and group sizes. You may also find similar activities within different chapters, so that you have a range of activities to choose from within a particular context.

In relevant chapters in this book, you will find the following tables (Tables 1.2, 1.3), at the beginning and end of chapters, so practitioners can reflect upon topics and confidence at the beginning of the chapter, and review your position and any need to plan for further development at the end.

TABLE 1.2 Practice reflection

Chapter sections	Fully engaged with strategies in place	Somewhat engaged	Further development needed
Thinking about families			
Families and values			
Reflective practice			
Seeing the setting with a positive lens			
What strategies are currently in place?			
What needs further development?			

TABLE 1.3 Practice review

Chapter section	Fully engaged with strategies in place	Somewhat engaged	Further development needed
Thinking about families			
Families and values			
Reflective practice			
Seeing the setting with a positive lens			
Reflection on chapter			
What changes have you made?			
What needs further development?			

Health check

Some of the activities in the pages ahead may be emotionally difficult for practitioners. Practitioners' own experiences will be uppermost and this can be painful when colleagues have had family challenges in their lives. It is important to offer an opt out of anything that touches too painfully on previous scars. You might want to talk to practitioners about how this may affect them. You are working with adults and their engagement is essential in order that learning will take place. This requires no more than an acknowledgement, which could look something like this:

> We hope that you enjoy working on some of these activities and reflecting on the development of your skills in relation to working with parents. As a manager, I want to make a judgement on how comfortable you are with each other and which activities you want to include. For some of the activities, there will be opportunities to share your recollections of your own childhood, in order to understand families from a range of different contexts. For some of you, who may have had unhappy family experiences, this may be difficult and possibly upsetting. Please be assured that there is nothing that you are required to share and if you feel uncomfortable at any point, please take a

break for a few moments. However, if you feel that there are issues that upset you and that have not been resolved, this may be the time to consider visiting your GP to discuss how you are affected. Your GP may be able to refer you to additional support.

Working as a training group in an early years setting

This book is intended as a self-help guide for settings, with an array of activities and photocopiable resources to use to support the professional development of the team. It is also worth adding that training skills are not part of the qualifications of early years managers, although of course there may be members of the team who are experienced trainers. You might be sharing the responsibilities of running training sessions, or you may be hiring a trainer to run some training sessions.

For those who have less experience, here are some useful points that everyone who is working with adults should take on board when they run training.

- There is a significant difference between working with a group of adults and working with a group of children. The learning environment should be in contrast (for the staff at your setting) to the environment that staff experienced when they were at school or College. According to Knowles *et al.* (2015), there are two different teaching/learning models: a *content model* and a *process model*, with the *process model* being most appropriate when working with adults, because it 'is concerned with providing procedures and resources for helping learners acquire information and skills' (Knowles *et al.*, 2015, p. 51). This is in contrast with the *content model* that solely transmits information and skills. The main way that this distinction can be seen is through the **preparation for learning** because when working with adults, the focus is on self-directed learning. In other words, the practitioners need to invest in the learning before it starts and therefore some preparation is essential and can have an impact on the engagement.
- Prepare participants by encouraging participation and engagement in the topic, explaining that the training depends on people sharing experiences, trusting each other, listening and respecting. Stress that no one will be made to divulge anything that they are not comfortable with.
- Think about the environment – the warmth, feel and comfort of the room will help people to relax and see this training as a positive event.
- Make the goals of the event clear, so colleagues know what to expect in advance. Participants need to be motivated to engage.

- Adopt a facilitating rather than a teaching role (Knowles *et al.*, 2015). This is because adults already have significant life experience and need to be able to share this with other members of the group.
- Group work can provide rich opportunities for learning – ensure there is plenty of flexibility when working with groups, and encourage them to share thoughts respectfully. This can be achieved through the setting of ground rules before any training starts.

Thinking about families

QUOTE FOR DISCUSSION OR REFLECTION

For any parental involvement practice to be considered meaningful, it should be a desirable practice; that is, it should be wanted, needed and liked by all three of the key stakeholders: teacher, parent and child.

(Zhang, 2015, p. 115)

Discuss the extent to which you agree with this, and whether it applies to practice in your setting.

Responsibilities of the early years practitioner

All early years settings, from childminders to 200 place day care centres, have a responsibility and a duty to work with parents and families (DfE, 2017). Many practitioners who have undertaken study in this area will be aware of the developmental opportunities that are enhanced through working with parents (Desforges & Abouchaar, 2003; Hoover-Dempsey *et al.*, 2005; Sylva *et al.*, 2004; Zhang, 2015). However, working with parents is as complex and varied as working with people.

For a number of reasons, a template – 'one size fits all' – does not represent the solution to working effectively with parents. Rather, practitioners have a responsibility to build individual and personalised relationships with parents as the transfer of care for the child creates a co-dependency that can blossom into a positive and constructive set of interactions only when trust and dependability is demonstrated from all those within the relationship. Those making use of childcare will be as diverse as it is possible to be in their personalities, beliefs, dispositions, income, socio-economic status, class, race, ethnicity, faith, sexual orientation, health and nationality. Some settings will be more diverse in aspects such as nationality, depending on the diversity of the area.

However, nationality/race/faith/ethnicity are perhaps the more obvious traits that can be seen, whereas, there are many more traits that can only be discovered through dialogue, friendly conversations, questioning and, most importantly, listening.

For practitioners, the use of reflection to identify their own values and attitudes is a prerequisite to successful engagement with parents. There are expectations that should be in place: the ability to reflect on own practice and make changes where needed; the ability to listen; an open-minded approach to all families; a disposition of friendliness and welcome. From these skills comes the development of a professional understanding of self and of the families with whom you are working.

Definitions

Parents

By the term 'parents' we mean anybody who has parental responsibility for young children and this term is intended to include carers, family members who are taking parental responsibility. This book is aimed in particular at those working and caring for the under-5s (those working within the Early Years Foundation Stage), though much of the content and activities will still be relevant for those caring for older children.

Families

By the term 'families' we mean anybody who is in a social unit where some members are caring for children. Many families share parenting responsibilities among themselves, according to the dynamics and construction of the group and these responsibilities may include delivering children to a setting, helping them with their learning at home or liaising with practitioners. It cannot be assumed that the main carer will always be the same person – families may have a number of people who are responsible in different ways for caring for children. Family units may also consist of individuals who are not part of the family unit by partnership. Many family groupings also include close friends who, by dint of the proximity of the relationship, would consider themselves (and be considered by others) to be part of the family.

Starting points

One way to start the conversation about working with parents, carers and families is through the discussion of families within the setting – practitioners' own families. This will help to develop a level of understanding about the range of families, experiences, cultures, values and beliefs. It will also help to embed the principles of trusting, tolerant relationships. Here are some activities to get staff talking about their families. You should read out the health check on page 4 before starting.

Longer activity: Families

You can use the photocopiable blank sheet (on the website) for individual or group work. Each practitioner should think about his or her own family and consider what makes them a family. There are the obvious factors such as family relationship but there are also less overt factors that make a family what they are. Once done, practitioners can share their own family picture with colleagues. Here is one example in Table 1.4. You'll find a blank table for your own use in the downloadable resources.

TABLE 1.4 My family: activity

My family	Fill in the boxes below:
Who are they?	*Mum, (dad died), brother and his family, two nephews, husband, two children, now grown up.*
What is their story? Add a little context here – are they ambitious, sporty, academic, high maintenance, all sorts?	*Varies from each branch of family – brother was the academic one while young, but now I'm doing my Foundation Degree! None of our children have gone on to University but there's still time! Lots of humour runs through the family – comes from my husband!*
What do I trust about them?	*Always there for me.*
What drives me mad about them?	*It's always me that gets people together.*
What wouldn't I change about them?	*I wouldn't change anything.*

Once you have completed this activity, share with a colleague or just reflect on the ways you have summarised your family. There are probably some good bits and some infuriating bits. Some people will be estranged from their blood family but have others who are as good as family, so the word family will mean different things to different people.

You can also complete this exercise using buttons or pebbles, for those who have a more visual learning style. This can be a strong exercise, as different buttons/pebbles are used to represent members of the family and this can sometimes raise issues.

This activity will help you to reflect on the various ways that families work and interact, and if you talk to others, you are likely to find that families do not all work in the same ways. Families are different. Another way that families are different is through their values. Values that come from families are quite hard to shake off as they have been part of people's lives since they were babies. This means that shaking off the value can also mean shaking off the family and that can be more than intended.

🕐 Longer activity: Values

We all bring values with us in our personal and professional lives. Every individual has a set of values, whether implicit or explicit. They are used when goals are set, decisions are made, and opinions are formed.

- Think of three values that you hold. This case study may help you to generate ideas:

> Sarah decided that her three important values were honesty, good manners, and the importance of human rights. When she thought about where they came from, she realised that her mum had always taught her to tell the truth when she was a child, and if her mum was cross with her for doing something wrong, she knew that she would be less cross than if she found out she had been lying! Then she remembered that her primary school used golden rules where everyone was encouraged to be kind to each other and say please and thank you and she remembered how much she liked it when someone said thank you to her. Finally, when she completed her early years qualification, she learned about children's rights and how important they were so she maintained that she would always work towards all children enjoying basic rights. Through her course and talking to other students, she developed a belief that just because children are younger does not mean they should not enjoy the freedoms and entitlements that rights can bring.
>
> (Wilson, 2016, p. 29)

- Notice where your values have come from – your family? Community or cultural beliefs beyond your family? Your own experiences? Think about whether you have discarded some values that you had as a child, but kept others. Why? Share in pairs – notice similarities and differences.
- Try to think beyond describing your values, but really work out why these values were, or are, important to you.
- Also, consider whether you found it easy to dismiss the values that are embedded within your family or culture. Sometimes values are so much part of a family that it is difficult to look at them objectively.
- Share the values with a partner and see whether they coincide.
- Agree with your partner about what those values say about each other. Was it easy to come to a decision? Did you agree? For example, in the case study above we could say that Sarah's values indicate that she is very people-centred and those values cross from her personal to her professional life.

We are exploring the topic of values again in the next activity:

Longer activity: Family values

Now look at this exercise where we look specifically at the values that you were raised with, and the extent to which you accept the views of others (Table 1.5). This sheet is to be completed individually and then discussed together at the end.

TABLE 1.5 Values: activity

Value	Extent to which you agree with your family (1–5 with 5 as completely agreeing)	Extent to which you are able to accept differing views (1–5 with 5 as completely accepting)
LGBT acceptance		
Divorce		
Children's behaviour		
Gender expectations		
Punishment/ reprimands		
Education		
Marriage		
Immigration		
Brexit		

Questions to explore with the group

- What did you find? Were your views quite close to those of your family? This is not unusual as our formative experiences can be hard to shake off.
- What about your tolerance of differing views? Is this difficult? Do strong views that you don't feel comfortable with make you defensive, angry even?
- Would you get more cross with views held by your family than with your colleague, say? Why do you think that is?
- What happens when your values clash with those of a parent?

Partnership with parents/parental engagement/ parental involvement

There is considerable research already undertaken into the definitions and values of these terms. The phrase 'partnership working' is used in the EYFS *Statutory Framework* (DfE, 2017) and it is intended to mean any interaction between parents and practitioners in relation to the wellbeing and education of children.

Parental engagement and parental involvement are often used interchangeably although some researchers categorises them as two different levels of engagement (Goodall & Montgomery, 2014). For the purposes of this toolkit, the terms will be used very broadly and in order to represent the ways that practitioners and parents work together. Overall, it is accepted that parental involvement has a positive effect on children's outcomes. However, some would argue that the effects of parental involvement on children's achievements are 'inconclusive' (Edwards & Warin, 2010; Gorard & See, 2013). Edwards and Warin note that impact is not always measured so it is impossible to prove achievements directly related to parental involvement.

Key points to note:

- When working with parents be clear about your objectives and goals – and check that these correspond with the goals of parents, rather than this being an imposition on them.
- Take the family's cultural norms and expectations into account, through listening to parents about their own education and expectations. This will avoid barriers building when your expectations are different. (See sections on listening to parents (p. 44), avoiding pre-judgments (p. 46)).
- One valuable way of thinking about practice and developing new ways of working is to use reflective practice.

Reflective practice

It is important to use reflection (both in practice and on practice, as exemplified by Schon, 1983) in order to make best use of this toolkit. The quickest way to describe it is to think of it as an exploration of practice. Those who do not fully apply the techniques of reflection might think about an element of practice and then decide that nothing needs to change. This is not reflection. It gives you nothing back and uses your time with little return. It can also indicate that there is a resistance to change and growth. Some practitioners are nervous about change because there may be an implication that they have done something wrong in the past – this too is not the purpose of reflection. There is no blame, there is no wrong, there is just growth and openness. The easiest way to build your expertise in this area is to mentally accept that there is nothing that does not need to change. This does not mean that everything you are doing is wrong, but it does mean that everything you are doing could be improved in some ways (even though you may decide that the changes are not a priority). It is hoped is that managers and room leaders value their own skills and knowledge and open themselves to growth and development, in recognition of the high achievements that they are already implementing.

☾ Overnight reflection: Gathering information

Reflection – what do you mean by reflection? Do some research into the meaning of the terms reflection-on-practice and reflection-in-practice (Schon, 1983) in relation to working with parents, and share some examples of when you have reflected in – and on – your practice.

Having spent some time thinking and reflecting on your practice, you may have been considering the ways in which practice and policy is implemented in your own setting. You have probably been thinking about how your setting works in relation to parents, and perhaps of some of the things that you have been meaning to do but not got around to yet. Looking at a setting from a positive perspective can also help you to see what goes on and how well you are doing. It can also help to remember that you are probably doing a good job – so in order to remember the positives, use this next activity as an opener for staff. It can remind everyone of the good job they are doing.

Looking at your setting with a positive lens

When you set out on a task to improve practice, it is very important that you bring the staff along with you. As a team working towards a set of goals, motivational leadership can generate enthusiasm and energy for change, whereas implied criticism is demotivating and disheartening. Use this training manual to celebrate the great achievements already in place in your setting at the beginning of any process of change. Aim to move from good to outstanding and take your staff with you.

Longer activity: What is great about your setting?

Start with a short activity to highlight all the great things that you are doing as a setting, get staff into pairs or threes, with some post-it© notes, and ask them the questions in Table 1.6:

TABLE 1.6 What is great about your setting? activity

Staff room activity: What is great about your setting?
How do you champion parents and ensure they have a positive experience with you?
Use post-it© notes to identify all the positives about how your setting works with parents

You can develop this into a longer discussion:

- Put post-it© notes onto a large sheet of A2 paper
- Once all the post-it© notes are on the sheet, move them about so that they are divided into categories, for example, you may have responses about methods of communication; open days, space to talk to parents; parents engagement in the setting.
- Once you have the post-it© notes into categories, ask pairs in the group to take one of the categories and agree what skills have been needed to achieve these things.
- After short discussions, each group feeds the skills used to achieve the outcomes. This is a celebration of the talent that is in place in the setting. The trainer should recognise the existing skills.

Once you have celebrated the undoubted skills and qualities of your setting, use this next activity to adjust your lens yet again and just start to look at the setting from the perspective of the parents.

⏱ Longer activity: Sensory experiences

In small groups, give each group this sheet and ask them to think about the sensory experiences of a new parent when they come into the nursery (Table 1.7).

- Complete the activity in small groups
- Feedback to main group
- Discuss the overall sensory experience for a parent – is there anything to think further about?

RESOURCES **TABLE 1.7** What do parents see? activity

Put yourself in the shoes of a prospective parent:
What do they see?
What do they smell?
What do they hear?
What do they feel?
What do they say and what is said to them?

Review of Chapter 1

By the end of this chapter you will have had a chance to think about how your setting works with parents and you will have carried out a couple of sessions with your staff. You will hopefully have picked up some clues on where staff feel they are in terms of parental involvement, with strengths and areas for improvement identified. As a final closure to this chapter, complete Table 1.8 and see whether your results, reflections and comments have changed from when you started the chapter.

TABLE 1.8 Practice review

Chapter section	Fully engaged with strategies in place	Somewhat engaged	Further development needed
Thinking about families			
Families and values			
Reflective practice			
Seeing the setting with a positive lens			
Reflection on chapter			
What changes have you made?			
What needs further development?			

References

Children's Workforce Development Council (CWDC). (2010). *Families going forward learner resources*. Available: http://webarchive.nationalarchives.gov.uk/20111108140857/ http://shortbreakcarers.cwdcouncil.org.uk/families-going-forward-learner-resources

Department for Education (DfE) (2017). *Statutory framework for the early years foundation stage*. London: DfE.

Desforges, C. & Abouchaar, A. (2003). *The impact of parental involvement, parental support and family education on pupil achievements and adjustment: A literature review, RR433*. Nottingham: DfES.

Edwards, A. & Warin, J. (2010). Parental involvement in raising the achievement of primary school pupils: Why bother? *Oxford Review of Education, 25* (3), 325–341.

Goodall, J. & Montgomery, C. (2014). Parental involvement to parental engagement: A continuum, *Educational Review, 66*(4), 399–410.

Gorard, S. & See, B.H. (2013). *Do parental involvement interventions increase attainment? A review of the evidence*. London: Nuffield Foundation. www.nuffieldfoundation.org/sites/ default/files/files/Do_parental_involvement_interventions_increase_attainment1.pdf

Hoover Dempsey, K. V., Walker, J. M. T., Sandler, H.M., Whetsel, D., Green, C.L., Wilkins, A.S., & Closson, K. (2005). Why do parents become involved? Research findings and implications. *The Elementary School Journal, 106* (2), 105–130.

Knowles, M.S., Holton, E.F III, & Swanson, R.A. (2015). *The adult learner: The definitive classic in adult learning and human resource development. Eighth education*. Abingdon: Routledge.

National College for Teaching and Leadership (NCTL) (2013). *Teachers' standards (early years)*. Retrieved from: https://www.gov.uk/government/uploads/system/uploads/attachment_data/file/ 211646/Early_Years_Teachers__Standards.pdf

Office for Standards in Education (Ofsted) (2018). *Early years inspection handbook*. London: Ofsted.

Pirchio, S., Tritrini, C., Passiatore, Y., & Taeschner, T. (2013). The role of the relationship between parents and educators for child behaviour and wellbeing. *International Journal about Parents in Education, 7*, (2), 145–155.

Schon, D. (1983). *The reflective practitioner: How professionals think in action*. London: Temple Smith.

Sylva, K., Melhuish, E., Sammons, P., Siraj-Blatchford, I., & Taggart, B. (2004). *The effective provision of pre-school education (EPPE) Project Final Report. A longitudinal evaluation (1997–2004)*. London: DfES.

Wilson, T. (2016). *Working with parents, carers and families in the early years*. Oxon: Routledge.

Zhang, Q. (2015). Defining 'meaningfulness': Enabling preschoolers to get the most out of parental involvement. *Australasian Journal of Early Childhood, 40* (4), 112–120.

Policy, frameworks and the production of effective paperwork

TABLE 2.1 Links to EY documentation

Teachers' Standards (Early Years), (NCTL, 2013)	Early years inspection handbook (Ofsted, updated 2018)	*Statutory framework for early years foundation stage (DfE, 2017)*
4.5 6.1 8.6 7.3		3.7

In the last chapter, we introduced the rationale for this toolkit and started to use a range of activities and exercises to help understand the practitioner's own perspective in order to understand those of other families. This chapter links the principles of effective partnership practice with required documentation, so looks in particular at the *Statutory Framework for the Early Years Foundation Stage* (DfE, 2017) and Ofsted Inspection requirements (Ofsted, 2015a; 2015b). This chapter will support setting leads in a review of their paperwork in this area, for example, identification of the required documents in order to be compliant with the *Statutory Framework for the Early Years Foundation Stage*; two-year-old check (Table 2.2). You will find up-to-date information and guidance, with links to other sources, on the Foundation Years website (www.foundationyears.org.uk/eyfs-statutory-framework/).

TABLE 2.2 Practice reflection

Chapter section	Fully engaged with strategies in place	Somewhat engaged	Further development needed
Statutory Framework for EYFS			
Ofsted *Early Years Inspection*			
What strategies are currently in place?			
What needs further development?			

☾ Overnight reflection: Applying the EYFS

How do you use the EYFS in relation to your partnership work? How useful is it and how confident do you feel of your EYFS knowledge and the requirements relating to partnership?

Required documentation and partnership work: EYFS

There are two main documents that we shall look at in this chapter, as they include statutory regulation (EYFS *Statutory Framework* and Ofsted *Early Years Inspection Handbook*). This will allow you to work out how you can evidence required documentation, although there are many more documents out there, for example, the non-statutory guidance, *Development Matters* (Early Education, 2012), to offer additional information.

Early Years Foundation Stage Statutory Framework (DfE, 2017)

First, the underpinning regulations for all registered early years settings: Early Years Foundation Stage Statutory Framework (EYFSSF) can be found here: www.foundationyears.org.uk/files/2017/03/EYFS_STATUTORY_FRAMEWORK_2017.pdf

The document was simplified and shortened (latest version 2017) and now it is 37 pages long. Its contents are required practice in 'maintained schools; non-maintained schools; independent schools; all providers on the Early Years Register; and all providers registered with an early years childminder agency' (DfE, 2017, p. 3). Its purpose is to provide a framework of practice for all settings, whether nursery, childminder setting, school (maintained, non-maintained or independent) and in particular to provide:

- quality and consistency
- a secure foundation
- partnership working
- equality of opportunity (DfE, 2017, p. 5).

As one of the four cornerstones of the document, the provision of **partnership working** is clearly something that needs to be transparent and visible within a setting's underpinning ethos.

On page 6, the overarching themes of the EYFS are stated:

Longer activity: Overarching themes of the EYFS

TABLE 2.3 Themes of the EYFS: activity

Unique child
Positive relationships
Enabling environments
Learning and development

Source: DfE, 2017.

Look at the four themes in Table 2.3 – you have probably looked at them hundreds of times during training and development work. Think about the themes from a parents' perspective. Why might they be important for parents? Take each theme in turn and add some notes to the Table 2.3.

Sections of the EYFS

In **section 1**, the requirements of what settings must do in terms of learning and development are laid out, structured by the seven areas of learning and development.

The early learning goals reflect the attainment of children by the time they reach the end of the EYFS and this is assessed through the EYFS profile. As all children develop at different rates, some will exceed the goals and some will not reach them; however, they are targets to be worked towards by most children, with the results fed into the next educational setting. (As we go to press, there are reports of a new reception class baseline assessment being introduced by autumn 2020.) There are 17 early learning goals.

In **section 2**, the Statutory Framework lays down the assessment requirements, which includes formative assessment (ongoing), the two years old progress check, and the final assessment of the EYFS: the Profile.

Section 3, the safeguarding and welfare requirements, includes expectations on staff qualifications, ratios as well as clarification of 'suitable people'.

Throughout the publication, there is an embedded requirement to work in partnership with parents. For example in Section 3 it is stated that:

> Providers must support staff to undertake appropriate training and professional development opportunities to ensure they offer quality learning and development experiences for children that continually improves.
>
> (DfE, 2017, p. 21).

By using this book, you can assert your commitment to staff training in relation to partnership work that supports children's learning and development.

All the expectations in relation to working with parents within the EYFS have been collated and added to Table 2.4. This can be printed off and made available to your staff. You could also print it off, laminate it and cut up the individual requirements so you can use them for activities and allow staff to work on separate requirements.

It is worth looking through the expectations initially, in order to gain an understanding of the messages given in this important statutory document.

Overarching principle:

Children learn and develop well in **enabling environments**, in which their experiences respond to their individual needs and there is a strong partnership between practitioners and parents and/or carers.

TABLE 2.4 Links to the EYFS and working with parents

Statutory Framework for the EYFS	Requirements that relate to working with parents
s. 1.6 p. 9	'if a child's progress in any prime area gives cause for concern, practitioners must discuss this with the child's parents and/or carers and agree how to support the child. Practitioners must consider whether a child may have a special educational need or disability which requires specialist support. They should link with, and help families to access, relevant services from other agencies as appropriate.'
s. 1.7 p. 9	'If a child does not have a strong grasp of English language, practitioners must explore the child's skills in the home language with parents and/or carers, to establish whether there is cause for concern about language delay.'
s. 1.10 p. 10	'Providers must inform parents and/or carers of the name of the key person, and explain their role, when a child starts attending a setting. The key person must help ensure that every child's learning and care is tailored to meet their individual needs. The key person must seek to engage and support parents and/or carers in guiding their child's development at home. They should also help families engage with more specialist support if appropriate.'

TABLE 2.4 *continued*

Statutory Framework for the EYFS	Requirements that relate to working with parents
s. 2.1 p.13	'In their interactions with children, practitioners should respond to their own day-to-day observations about children's progress and observations that parents and carers share.'
s. 2.2 p. 13	'Parents and/or carers should be kept up-to-date with their child's progress and development. Practitioners should address any learning and development needs in partnership with parents and/or carers, and any relevant professionals.'
s. 2.3 and s. 2.4 p. 13	'When a child is aged between two and three, practitioners must review their progress, and provide parents and/or carers with a short written summary of their child's development in the prime areas. This progress check must identify the child's strengths, and any areas where the child's progress is less than expected. If there are significant emerging concerns, or an identified special education need, practitioners should develop a targeted plan to support the child's future learning and development involving parents and/or carers and other professionals . . . 'Practitioners must discuss with parents and/or carers how the summary of development can be used to support learning at home.'
s. 2.5 p. 14	'Practitioners should encourage parents and/or carers to share information from the progress check with other relevant professionals, including their health visitor and the staff of any new provision the child may transfer to. Practitioners must agree with parents and/or carers when will be the most useful point to provide a summary. Where possible, the progress check and the Healthy Child Programme health and development review at age two (when health visitors gather information on a child's health and development) should inform each other and support integrated working. This will allow health and education professionals to identify strengths as well as any developmental delay and any particular support from which they think the child/family might benefit. Providers must have the consent of parents and/or carers to share information directly with other relevant professionals.'
s. 2.6 p. 14	'The Profile must reflect: ongoing observation; all relevant records held by the setting; discussions with parents and carers, and any other adults whom the teacher, parent or carer judges can offer a useful contribution.'
s. 2.9 p. 14	'Schools must share the results of the Profile with parents and/or carers, and explain to them when and how they can discuss the Profile with the teacher who completed it.'
s. 3.3 p.16	'Childminders are not required to have written policies and procedures. However, they must be able to explain their policies and procedures to parents, carers, and others (for example Ofsted inspectors or the childminder agency with which they are registered) and ensure any assistants follow them.'
s. 3.7 p. 17	'If providers have concerns about children's safety or welfare, they must notify agencies with statutory responsibilities without delay.'

continued

TABLE 2.4 *continued*

Statutory Framework for the EYFS	Requirements that relate to working with parents
s. 3.25 p. 22	'Providers should display (or make available to parents) staff PFA certificates or a list of staff who have a current PFA certificate.'
s. 3.27 p. 23	'The key person's role is to offer a settled relationship for the child and build a relationship with their parents.'
s. 3.28 p. 23	'Providers must inform parents and/or carers about staff deployment, and, when relevant and practical, aim to involve them in these decisions.'
s. 3.44 p. 27	'The provider must promote the good health of children attending the setting. They must have a procedure, discussed with parents and/or carers, for responding to children who are ill or infectious, take necessary steps to prevent the spread of infection, and take appropriate action if children are ill.'
s. 3.46 p. 27	'Medicine (both prescription and non-prescription) must only be administered to a child where written permission for that particular medicine has been obtained from the child's parent and/or carer. Providers must keep a written record each time a medicine is administered to a child, and inform the child's parents and/or carers on the same day, or as soon as reasonably practicable.'
s. 3.47 p.2 8	'Providers must record and act on information from parents and carers about a child's dietary needs.'
s. 3.50 p. 28	'Providers must inform parents and/or carers of any accident or injury sustained by the child on the same day as, or as soon as reasonably practicable after, and of any first aid treatment given.'
s. 3.52 p. 29	'Providers, including childminders, must keep a record of any occasion where physical intervention is used, and parents and/or carers must be informed on the same day, or as soon as reasonably practicable.'
s. 3.61 p. 30	'Providers must also ensure that there is an area where staff may talk to parents and/or carers confidentially.'
s. 3.62 p. 30	'Providers must only release children into the care of individuals who have been notified to the provider by the parent.'
s. 3.64 p. 31	'Providers must determine where it is helpful to make some written risk assessments in relation to specific issues, to inform staff practice, and to demonstrate how they are managing risks if asked by parents and/or carers or inspectors.'
s. 3.68 p. 31	'Providers must maintain records and obtain and share information (with parents and carers, other professionals working with the child, the police, social services and Ofsted or the childminder agency with which they are registered, as appropriate) to ensure the safe and efficient management of the setting, and to help ensure the needs of all children are met. Providers must enable a regular two-way flow of information with parents and/or carers, and between providers, if a child is attending more than one setting. If requested, providers should incorporate parents' and/or carers' comments into children's records.'

TABLE 2.4 *continued*

Statutory Framework for the EYFS	Requirements that relate to working with parents
s. 3.70 p. 32 s. 3.72 p. 32	'Parents and/or carers must be given access to all records about their child, provided that no relevant exemptions apply to their disclosure under the DPA.' 'Providers must record the following information for each child in their care: full name; date of birth; name and address of every parent and/or carer who is known to the provider (and information about any other person who has parental responsibility for the child); which parent(s) and/or carer(s) the child normally lives with; and emergency contact details for parents and/or carers.'
s. 3.73 p. 32	'Providers must make the following information available to parents and/or carers: • how the EYFS is being delivered in the setting, and how parents and/or carers can access more information • the range and type of activities and experiences provided for children, the daily routines of the setting, and how parents and carers can share learning at home • how the setting supports children with special educational needs and disabilities • food and drinks provided for children • details of the provider's policies and procedures (all providers except childminders (see paragraph 3.3) must make copies available on request) including the procedure to be followed in the event of a parent and/or carer failing to collect a child at the appointed time, or in the event of a child going missing at, or away from, the setting • staffing in the setting; the name of their child's key person and their role; and a telephone number for parents and/or carers to contact in an emergency.'
s. 3.74 p. 33	'Providers must put in place a written procedure for dealing with concerns and complaints from parents and/or carers, and must keep a written record of any complaints, and their outcome.' [see additional information re childminders.]
s. 3.75 p. 33	'Providers must make available to parents and/or carers details about how to contact Ofsted or the childminder agency with which the provider is registered as appropriate, if they believe the provider is not meeting the EYFS requirements. If providers become aware that they are to be inspected by Ofsted or have a quality assurance visit by the childminder agency, they must notify parents and/or carers. After an inspection by Ofsted or a quality assurance visit by their childminder agency, providers must supply a copy of the report to parents and/or carers of children attending on a regular basis.'
s. 3.76 p. 34	'Providers must hold their certificate of registration (which must be displayed at the setting and shown to parents and/or carers on request).'

Table 2.4 includes all references to parents within the current *Statutory Framework* of the EYFS (DfE, 2017). Some of them are very general references, stating the need to discuss development with parents, for example. Others make specific stipulations, for example displaying the certificate of registration, keeping a record of complaints, etc. These requirements can be developed through efficient office management and maintenance of paperwork. In contrast, this is a more complex statement:

> s. 3.27: 'The key person's role is to offer a settled relationship for the child and build a relationship with their parents.'

> (DfE, 2017, p. 23)

This single sentence contains within it one of the most complex aspects of working in partnerships with parents, so when looking at the *Statutory Framework*, be aware that different statements require different levels of engagement and reflection.

You will find that Table 2.4 includes all the sections of the EYFS where parents or partnership is mentioned. You can select which ones you want to work on during staff training sessions. There are ways you can work together with practitioners on this document.

- print out a number of copies of Table 2.4 for staff to share and discuss in groups;
- print off the table and laminate the pages, then cut out the individual sections so you can move them around;
- plan a workshop – see activity below.

Here are some ideas for a workshop:

Longer activity 1

Small groups choose one of the EYFS sections for a requirement for a written procedure and reviews documentation for that area, e.g.:

s. 3.74 p. 33	'Providers must put in place a written procedure for dealing with concerns and complaints from parents and/or carers, and must keep a written record of any complaints, and their outcome.'

Or

s. 1.6 p. 9	'if a child's progress in any prime area gives cause for concern, practitioners must discuss this with the child's parents and/or carers and agree how to support the child. Practitioners must consider whether a child may have a special educational need or disability which requires specialist support. They should link with, and help families to access, relevant services from other agencies as appropriate.'

TABLE 2.5 Meeting statutory requirements in your setting: activity

• Find existing documentation on the requirement that is used in the setting
• Discuss whether it needs updating
• Discuss whether practitioners know about this
• Suggest areas for updating
• Set date for completion of update

The tasks in Table 2.5 will have the dual benefit of increasing staff awareness of current documentation in your setting, and having some ownership of the wording and updating of the documentation. You may want to carry this out with the leadership team.

Longer activity 2: Pick and mix – each member of the group chooses a laminated section at random, e.g.

30 3.61	Providers must also ensure that there is an area where staff may talk to parents and/or carers confidentially.

- In pairs, discuss how this happens in the setting, and identifies whether it is:
  - requirement fully in place
  - requirement generally in place
  - requirement not in place
- The pair then feeds back their view to the main group, and the decision is made whether this already fully meets requirements.
- If not, the pairs agree to write down some ideas of actions to be taken, which are taken on for review by the senior management. In this way, staff have the opportunity to share ideas and management and practitioners work together.

Required documentation and partnership work: Ofsted *Early Years Inspection Handbook* (Ofsted, 2018)

Possible outcomes from inspections are:

- grade 1: outstanding
- grade 2: good

- grade 3: requires improvement
- grade 4: inadequate.

You can find more information here: www.gov.uk/government/organisations/ofsted

The Ofsted *Early Years Inspection Handbook* offers guidance to inspectors and setting managers on the main expectations when carrying out an Ofsted inspection (Ofsted, 2018). The *Common Inspection Framework: Education, skills and early years* (2015) refers to the *Early Years Inspection Handbook* for guidance on inspections in early years settings. For example, Part 1 (How early years providers will be inspected), states:

> The provider must demonstrate how they will:
>
> - meet the learning and development requirements
> - meet the safeguarding and welfare requirements
> - develop and deliver the educational programmes
> - identify children's starting points and ensure that children make progress in their learning through effective planning, observation and assessment
> - safeguard children
> - **work in partnership with parents, carers and others**
> - offer an inclusive service
> - evaluate their service and strive for continuous improvement.
>
> (Ofsted, 2018, p. 6)

This links back to the EYFS *Statutory Framework* (DfE, 2017), so it would be worth considering how you can demonstrate the bullet points above, especially the emboldened partnership one. During an Ofsted inspection, the inspector/s will want to speak to parents to discuss how the setting discharges its duties (Ofsted, 2018, p. 17). Section 80 states that:

> Wherever possible, the inspector must seek the views of parents during the inspection, including any parents who ask to speak to them. This will contribute to judgements about how well the provision works in partnership with parents to support children's learning and development and the promotion of their wellbeing.

Section 81 continues:

> If the setting has been notified in advance, parents will know that an inspection is taking place. If most children arrive at, or are collected from, the provision at one time, the inspector should set aside time to speak to parents. The inspector must make sure that opportunities for speaking to them are not missed.

And section 82:

> If the timing of the inspection means it is not possible to gain parents' views directly, **the inspector must check how the provider obtains and uses their views to improve its service. If there is no evidence relating to this, the** inspector must consider whether the partnership with parents is good enough.
>
> (pp. 17–18)

In other words, if there is only weak, anecdotal evidence of seeking parents' views, the whole question of effective partnership may be doubted.

☾ Overnight reflection: Seeking parents' views

Identify some examples of how you have sought the views of parents and used them to improve the service offered to families.

When the staff team meet, you can use this overnight reflection as an opening activity to explore the ways that practitioners gather the views of parents (Table 2.6).

TABLE 2.6 Gathering the views of parents: activity

Method for gathering views	Topic	Evidence
Example: Survey	Example: Online survey to parents about preferred method of spending time with the key person BA Education student's survey on school readiness	Copies of all survey responses kept in shared drive/filing cabinet in office (kept locked)
Survey		
Response to posters in setting		
Email		
Response to newsletter		
Twitter comment		
Tapestry		
Meeting		

Use the downloadable version of this form, which you can adapt to include your own methods of gathering views. Once you have completed this activity, you will be able to see a) whether you have evidence of gathering opinions from parents and whether there are any gaps that need to be addressed.

Gathering views from parents – ethical considerations

The information that you may gather from parents can be gained in a variety of ways (see Table 2.6 and think about what happens in your own setting). There are ethical considerations to be taken into account, especially in the light of the new data protection legislation that came into effect in May 2018 (the General Data Protection Register) and included in any formal gathering of information, though, and you should be sure that you comply with required ethical procedures, for example:

- always explain why you want this information and what you will be using it for;
- never use information gathered for purposes other than the ones stated at the outset;
- respect confidentiality: never discuss parents' views given in confidence unless you have express permission to do;
- don't keep information for longer than you need to.

It may be prudent to produce a consent letter for the setting's welcome pack, explaining to parents that you might want to collect information that reflects their views. The Pre-School Learning Alliance has some useful guidance on their website: www.pre-school.org.uk/preparing-your-early-years-setting-gdpr

Inspectors' judgements and what they are based on:

s. 146 (Ofsted, 2018, p. 29) states that:

> 'Inspectors should take account of all the judgements made across the evaluation schedule. In particular, they should consider:
>
> - the progress all children make in their learning and development relative to their starting points and their readiness for the next stage of their education including, where appropriate, readiness for school
> - the extent to which the learning and care that the setting provides meet the needs of the range of children who attend, including disabled children and those who have special educational needs
> - children's personal and emotional development, including whether they feel safe and are secure and happy

- whether the requirements for children's safeguarding and welfare have been fully met and there is a **shared understanding of and responsibility** for protecting children
- the effectiveness of leadership and management in evaluating practice and securing continuous improvement that improves children's life chances.'

So whilst inspectors will be focusing on the elements above, there are four categories where **parents' views** will be taken into account:

- effectiveness of the leadership and management;
- quality of teaching, learning and assessment;
- personal development, behaviour and welfare;
- outcomes for children.

For example, in the overall effectiveness of leadership and management, the judgement made will include the extent to which leaders, managers and governors (Ofsted, 2018, p. 30):

s. 148 p.30	'evaluate the quality of the provision and outcomes through robust self-evaluation, taking account of the views of parents and children, and use the findings to develop capacity for sustainable improvement.'

Clearly, the principles of partnership practice are incorporated in this Inspection Framework and it is imperative for settings to have robust evidence that demonstrates their engagement with parents. It is stated that evidence may be gathered through:

s. 151 p.32	'the effectiveness of self-evaluation, including contributions from parents, carers and other stakeholders.'
s. 151 p.32	'whether leaders have implemented well-focused improvement plans through engagement with staff, children, parents and carers.'
s. 151 p.32	'the effectiveness of arrangements for sharing information and working in partnership with other providers, schools and professionals to identify all children's needs and help them to make good progress.'

[NB As we go to press, the self-evaluation form is being abolished.]

It also takes into account the monitoring of any additional support needs:

s. 151 p. 32	'The effectiveness of the monitoring of children's progress, and interventions where needed, to ensure that gaps are narrowing for groups of children or individual children identified as being in need of support.'

The engagement with parents is also taken into consideration when assessing the quality of teaching, learning and assessment (s.154, p. 35). 'Inspectors will make a judgement on the effectiveness of teaching, learning and assessment by evaluating the extent to which:

s. 154 p.35	assessment information is gathered from looking at what children already know, understand and can do, and is informed by their parents and previous providers as appropriate.'
s. 154 p.35	'children understand how to develop as a result of regular interaction and encouragement from staff, and parents understand how their children should progress and how they can contribute to this.'
s. 154 p.35	'information for parents helps them to understand how children are doing in relation to their age and what they need to.'

Evidence of the above can come from:

- assessment on entry, including parental contributions
- progress checks of two-year-olds (where applicable)
- formative assessments, including any parental contributions (Ofsted, 2018, p. 36)

and discussions with parents about:

- how often practitioners share a good-quality summary of their observations of children with the children's parents
- how and when parents are asked for information about their child's development (Ofsted, 2018, p. 37)

The section on personal development, behaviour and welfare also refers to the relationships with parents. The *Inspection Handbook* notes that evidence to support this aspect of children's development might include:

'discussions with practitioners, children and parents and with managers about the key person system.' (s. 159, p. 40)

In addition:

> Although attendance at the setting is not mandatory providers should be
> alert to patterns of absence that may indicate wider safeguarding concerns.
> **Inspectors will explore how well providers work with parents** to promote
> children's good attendance especially the attendance of children for whom
> the provider receives the early years pupil premium.
>
> (s. 160, p. 40)

Longer activity: Evidence audit

In the previous paragraphs, there are a number of sections that relate to the
requirements of an Ofsted inspection. All of them are points for reflection and,
depending on your setting, this may be best taking place within the management team
or in the first instance as an individual manager's reflective activity.

Meeting the grade descriptors

As you look at the grade descriptors for teaching, learning and assessment, the high
priority given to seeking strategies to engage all parents is clear:

Outstanding:

- Highly successful strategies engage parents, **including those from different groups,**
  in their children's learning, both in the setting and at home. (Ofsted, 2018, p. 38)

Good:

- The key person system works effectively to engage parents, including those
  who may be more reluctant to contribute, in their children's learning. Parents
  contribute to initial assessments of children's starting points on entry and they
  are kept well informed about their children's progress. Parents are encouraged
  to support and share information about their children's learning and
  development at home.

Impact

As part of the Ofsted inspection, inspectors will make judgments on the setting's partnership with parents (Ofsted, 2018, p. 17).

Reflect on how you are gathering evidence of impact.

- Are you asking parents what they are doing differently because of their engagement with the setting?
- Is there documentation showing partnership work and the effect it has had on a child or a family?
- Could you create some case studies where the partnership has been successful?

Reviewing previous reports

The Report will then identify the ways that the setting needs to improve and additionally report in further detail against the following headings:

- Effectiveness of the leadership and management
- Quality of teaching, learning and assessment
- Personal development, behaviour and welfare
- Outcomes for children.

The significance of the Ofsted Report is well understood by managers and practitioners in settings. At the worst outcome, a setting may be closed because of poor adherence to the regulatory requirements. At best, the provision can increase its status, popularity with local users and in consequence increase its income substantially. The Ofsted logo is used on websites and documentation as a badge of quality across the UK, and in this sense there is no better-known quality assurance sign.

It is important to make detailed use of your current report in order to review points for development and make explicit reference to the ways that you have changed practice.

Aiming for outstanding Ofsted status

There may be many ways in which your setting is working at an outstanding level, but if you are not evidencing your practice, you will not be successful in persuading the Ofsted Inspector that this is the case. When considering the relationships that you build with families, you will find that there are many opportunities to gather and retain evidence. There are many guides available online that will offer you help in becoming an 'outstanding' setting, for example:

http://blog.optimus-education.com/21-steps-achieving-outstanding–early–years–ofsted–judgement

www.pre-school.org.uk/sites/default/files/preparing_for_an_ofsted_inspection.pdf

These will take you through the expectations of all members of staff and across all areas in preparation for an inspection. Inspectors will want to talk to parents as well as gather data from questionnaires sent out to parents, so their evidence will come from both talking to parents and also from documentary evidence of their involvement. One key aspect to remember is that the engagement is in order to enhance the progress of children. Simply having good relationships will not take you to an outstanding judgement although applying that information to the work that takes place, and recording it, will be considered much more favourably.

Use this case study to consider the ways to improve a setting and to manage the challenging dynamics that can sometimes take place in a work environment. You can also go to the Ofsted website and look at Ofsted published reports, to see examples of partnership work:

https://reports.ofsted.gov.uk/

CASE STUDY

Jasmine is the Owner/Manager of a small, independent setting that has 50 registered places. This is her first managerial role and she has inherited some chaotic paperwork from the previous owner, so is creating a new system of record keeping from scratch. She has a distributive leadership style and wants her management team of deputy manager, SENCO and room leaders to have an active involvement in the new processes; however, the Deputy Manager is resistant to change, as she worked with the previous manager for some years. This puts her at odds with the newly appointed

continued

SENCO and some of the room leaders. Jasmine is aware that this is a sensitive situation and wants to move slowly, but she knows that Ofsted could visit at any time and that the paperwork has to be in place before any visit.

She sets up a meeting of the management team, but she meets up with the Deputy beforehand to assure her of her support and to ask for her engagement with the changes. She does this a week before the meeting because, although the time is tight, she feels that the DM needs time to adjust to the changes that she might be making and wants her to mentally prepare for a potentially difficult meeting. The DM appears to appreciate her support.

At the meeting, the Manager indicates that a weak area in the previous Ofsted report was the partnership with parents and that this is where the focus should lie. She notes that in the *Statutory Framework* of the EYFS, there is a requirement that 'providers must enable a regular two-way flow of information with parents and/or carers and between providers, if the child is attending more than one setting' (DfE, 2017, p. 32, s3.68). The Deputy becomes very defensive at this point and states that there is no point in involving other settings because they 'can't be bothered anyway'. The new SENCO disagrees that this is the case.

Jasmine needs to come away from this meeting with a robust provisional plan that she can work on. She needs to consider the following.

- **How can she bring the DM back onside during the meeting?**

- **How can she get the team to discuss what needs to be done (the identification of where the two-way flow takes place and whether records are maintained) in a positive way?**

- **What paperwork should be agreed upon in the meeting in order that all members of staff can leave with a strong understanding of the next steps to be completed?**

Finally, review your own latest Ofsted report to review the areas needed for improvement and work with the team on your action plan (Table 2.7).

TABLE 2.7 Practice review

Chapter section	Fully engaged with strategies in place	Somewhat engaged	Further development needed
Statutory Framework for the EYFS			
Ofsted *Early Years Inspection*			
Reflection on chapter			
What changes have you made?			
What needs further development?			

References

Department for Education (DfE) (2017). *Statutory framework for the early years foundation stage: Setting the standards for learning, development and care for children from birth to five.* London: DfE

Early Education. (2012). Development Matters. www.early-education.org.uk.

National College for Teaching and Leadership (NCTL) (2013). *Teachers' standards (early years).* Retrieved from: https://www.gov.uk/government/uploads/system/uploads/attachment_data/file/211646/Early_Years_Teachers__Standards.pdf

Office for Standards in Education (Ofsted). (2015). *Common inspection framework: Education, skills and early years.* London: Ofsted.

Office for Standards in Education (Ofsted) (2018). *Early years inspection handbook.* London: Ofsted.

3 | Breaking down barriers

TABLE 3.1 Links to EY documentation

Teachers' Standards (Early Years), (NCTL, 2013)	Early years inspection handbook (Ofsted, updated 2018)	*Statutory framework for early years foundation stage (DfE, 2017)*
2.7 8.6	s. 156 p. 37	s. 3.27 p. 23

Breaking down barriers

In order to work in partnership with all parents, some awareness and reflection on the potential barriers that can impede effective engagement between parents and practitioners is necessary. This chapter will encourage you to reflect on what you are already doing and introduce you to some opportunities to think beyond your current practice and develop trust-building activities that will work for your setting (Table 3.2).

We shall look at different activities that consider:

- Identifying barriers and developing a sharing culture
- Ways of listening to parents
- Understanding families and using strengths-based practice

TABLE 3.2 Practice reflection

Chapter section	Fully engaged with strategies in place	Somewhat engaged	Further development needed
Identifying barriers			
Ways of listening			
Families and strengths based practice			
What strategies are currently in place?			
What needs further development?			

Overnight reflection

All participants should complete this before starting the chapter in order to establish a starting position. You will return to this question in the chapter review, considering any changes in position or knowledge and understanding that you may have experienced after reading the chapter.

What is your starting position in terms of the barriers that might impede engagement between families and settings? First of all, spend some time thinking about your own experiences of school, any time you spent overseas where you did not understand the language, any time where you were dealing with a larger organisation. How did your confidence grow? What did people do to make you feel that you fitted in with them? What was it that made the difference, if anything?

During the following activities, think about the key factors that recur. Can you summarise the main causes of barriers in your setting?

Identifying barriers and developing a sharing culture

In order to break down barriers, it is necessary to reflect upon the places where the barriers might exist. Figure 3.1 illustrates the inter-relationship between setting, parents and children. Relationships between members of that triad can vary.

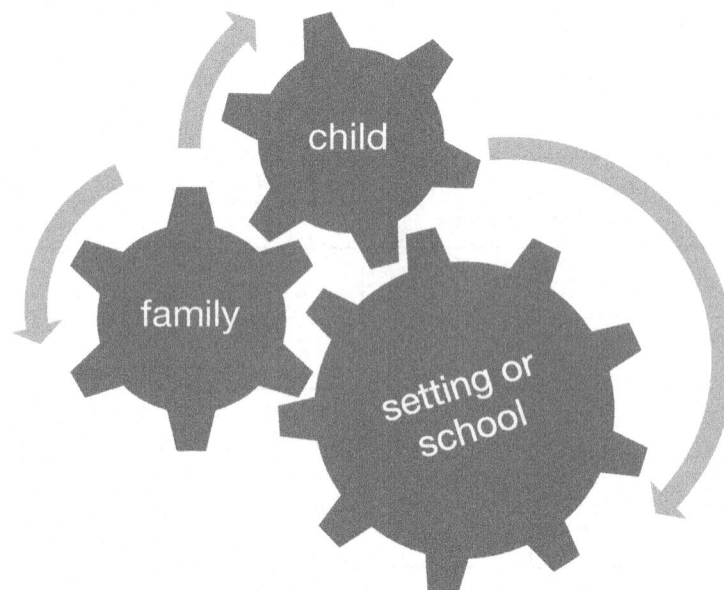

FIGURE 3.1 Interlocking relationships

The child should be the central point in all relationships but without the free movement of information that can be analysed, contextualised and triangulated, the picture remains incomplete.

Barriers

In settings, it can sometimes be hard to recognise the barriers that exist. In a busy environment where the necessity for routines, procedures and structure are a given, it is easy to forget that those who are new and unfamiliar to the structure and expectations (some of them perhaps implicit?) might find it difficult to communicate their anxiety. Alternatively, it is important to remember that engagement in a child's education is not always visible; in fact, most of the important partnership work is done at home. If you can find ways to build relationships and thereby unlock effective communication so that you can share engagement with the parent, then these barriers may be easier to dismantle.

Otherness and belongingness

Class, ethnicity, ideology, culture, values – a distinction in beliefs in relation to education – could set a family apart from the dominant ideologies of the setting. It has been argued that the level of involvement can be affected by a range of factors that are embedded in a family's cultural identity and expectation of the benefits of education to children's outcomes (Kremer-Sadlik & Fatigante, 2015).

So a sign of respect for teachers from one party could be misinterpreted as lack of engagement by the other and create a barrier.

Language barriers

Information sharing can be more limited if the family feels anxious about the information that they share.

> Some immigrant families with emergent language skills may fear that there is a chance that they are not properly documented to be in the country. [This situation] is likely to cause fear and anxiety, which lead to a lack of willingness to communicate openly and trustingly.
>
> (Byrd, 2012, p. 51)

Power balance

> There is a tendency, in considering the role of power in home–school relations, to assume that the differentials favour the teacher, who is the professional or 'expert' by virtue of her qualifications and knowledge of 'all children', as compared with the parent who is the expert only in her own child's development (and may even misconstrue or misunderstand that).
> . . . the reverse can [also] be true, and that parents who view themselves as 'professionals' may exercise power over practitioners whose professional qualifications they hold to be of little value.
>
> (Brooker, 2010, p. 184)

Discourse of exclusion

There are claims that models of partnership with parents lead to norms of 'white middle class expectation' (Whitmarsh, 2011, p. 538) and that partnership work does not translate easily to non-western contexts. 'A deficit discourse portrays particular parents, largely working-class, black, immigrant or sole parents, as failing to be good parents due to their inability to support their children in their learning as evident in their invisibility in schools' (Auerbach 1995, cited in Blackmore & Hutchison 2010, p. 501).

Parents' own school experiences

Parents whose own recollection of education and childhood was negative could find it difficult to feel comfortable in an educational environment: 'Parents' view of their role as a teacher and communicating with teachers and helping their children with school work, may, in part, be a result of their own educational experiences' (Kohl *et al.*, 2000, p. 2).

The following case studies can be used to discuss and consider a range of situations that might require patience, tolerance and creativity in approaches.

Longer activity: Three case studies

Download or photocopy these case studies, divide staff into three groups and assign one case study to each group. In groups, read and discuss the case study you have been assigned.

1. Alicia and Joshua believe that nurseries offer expert education and care and it is not up to them to give an opinion or become involved in their children's learning. They are attentive and diligent parents but do not see themselves as experts. They find it quite overwhelming to be asked what play activities they have been engaging in and whether they want to know more about the EYFS. They agree with their family that they may get something wrong and then get into trouble with the authorities.

2. Sarah and River are lesbian mothers of Jay and Conor, born through IVF, and who are now two and a half. They know that some of the parents talk about them and disapprove of the family set up, even though most parents are friendly when passing. Sarah and River want to feel more a part of the setting but as they both work, they do not know whether that is possible. Anna, the room leader in the toddler room, has heard a small minority of parents talking negatively about gay parents and how they would not allow their child to go to play at their houses and she hopes to avoid any children being affected by this as they get older.

3. Hannah is a primary school teacher who leaves her pre-school children in a local nursery. Anjana, her key person, finds her intimidating as she implies that she knows more than Anjana and in turn, Anjana secretly thinks that Hannah is right. This makes her feel uncomfortable about making suggestions and talking to Hannah about developmental issues.

As a group, discuss your cases and the ways that barriers can be broken down. Are there common factors? What are the distinguishing factors of each case? How can you use a positive approach with all of these? What is your role in each of these?

Here is another scenario for exploration. You could discuss this as a whole group or discuss in smaller groups and share your thoughts on the questions at the end.

CASE STUDY

Fadia has lived in the UK for 18 months. Her child, Sami, is 12 months old. Fadia has been suffering from postnatal depression and hopes that returning to work will improve her general wellbeing and reduce the depression. However, she is conflicted and torn about leaving her child, as she had promised her mother that she wouldn't adopt bad western habits such as leaving her children in order to pursue a career. Fadia's spoken English is reasonable but not perfect so she can miss nuances and colloquialisms. She is a private person who does not find sharing personal information easy. Fadia has been back at work for six weeks but Lisa, her key person, feels that she is not making progress at building a trusting relationship and she would like to broach some attachment issues that she has noticed with Sami. She really does not want to discuss these until she feels she knows Fadia better.

- **What barriers might limit communication here?**

- **How might Fadia be feeling?**

- **How would you approach this, given what you know and do not know?**

- **How can you relate this to everyday practice and draw some principles from it?**

Table 3.3 comprises a number of the factors that could create barriers and limit communication in a setting. This is not a comprehensive list and these will not all apply to all settings. Look at them, and consider:

- the relative value of them;
- which can be the most obstinate barriers?
- which can be overcome with relative ease?
- which do you feel confident about managing effectively?
- which would you call upon colleagues for help with?

TABLE 3.3 Barriers to communication: activity

Possible barriers	What do you think this means? Why would it be a barrier?	Rate the importance of this barrier (1–5)
Class and ethnicity		
Time		
Culture and values		
Health issues		
Sense of belonging		
Finance		
Ideology towards education		
Confidence – intimidation		
Work commitments, e.g. shift working		
Issues relating to separated parents		
Direction of communication		
Stress levels of practitioners and parents		
Unconscious bias		
Power balance		

Through the exploration of barriers from the parents' lens, it is easier to develop an empathy for those who find it harder to make connections with a setting. In the final section, there are some exercises to help practitioners and parents reduce the barriers and build effective, trusting relationships.

Listening to parents

You will have found activities relating to listening to parents throughout this book, because the act of listening is such a dominant feature of effective practice when working with families. Yet there are many examples of poor listening taking place, for understandable reasons such as lack of time, pressure of work, pressure of outside concerns and limited understanding of how much difference good listening can make. EVERYBODY likes to be listened to, to be felt that they are important and that their opinions and thoughts matter, are valued. So, partnership work starts through doing something that parents will like, even if what they are saying is: 'I'm too busy to talk to you!' Your active listening and understanding will progress the relationship, making it a wise investment of time that will pay off in the longer term, and it is an essential part of the skills set for practitioners working with parents.

One activity that can summarise the impact of effective, active listening is called: the good, the bad and the ugly.

Short activity: the good, the bad and the ugly!

Divide the group into sets of three and ensure that they are a distance apart from each other. They will take turns to be:

- a listener
- a speaker
- an observer.

Allocate them numbers: 1, 2 and 3 and tell them that they will takes turns to be a speaker for one minute. Cut these boxes out and give to the 1s, 2s and 3s respectively so they do not know what the others have written on their slip of paper (Table 3.4).

TABLE 3.4 The good, the bad, the ugly: activity

(1) to start by listening to (2), whilst (3) observes. (1) will listen with closed body language, virtual silence, looking around the room, clearly mind on something else. They will appear disinterested.
Then (2) will listen to (3), while (1) observes. (2) will listen and look very intensely at (3) but at every opportunity they will relate what the speaker is saying to their own experiences 'oh, I went there . . . what did you think' etc., butting into sentences with irrelevant anecdotes and looking over at other people and waving at them.
Then (3) will listen to (1), observed by (2). (3) will focus on the story, using body language to demonstrate engagement, nodding, occasionally paraphrasing or checking understanding. (3) does not lose attention but is warm and friendly and is actively listening so would be able to relate the whole story at the end.

After each member of the group has taken their turn, discuss how people felt when being ignored or feeling that someone was not listening, and how different the active listening felt. Observers should also feed into the discussion about the impact of the behaviour on the speaker.

Listening can also take place with a number of media, such as inviting parents to participate in surveys, putting up posters inviting their views. Make sure that you let parents know that you are listening to them through different methods, so you can capture all voices, not just the most vocal ones (Table 3.5).

TABLE 3.5 Signals that you value parents: activity

What signals do you give out to parents so that they know you value them?	
Tick the following if you have done this in the last week:	Tick?
• Greeted them by name	
• Followed on from a previous conversation	
• Remembered something that they were worried about and asked them about it	
• Learned some words in their language	
• Made signs in the nursery that reflect their language	
• Listened to them in detail	
• Followed their cultural/religious traditions within the nursery	
• Ensured that staff members are assigned to them who speak the same language	
• Found out more about them every time you see them	
• Welcomed members of the extended family	
• Asked them about their preferences	
• Tried to understand if they have been late	
• Told them about their child's achievements during the day	

Understanding families and strengths-based practice

Parents may have a number of conflicts in their lives when they are managing work and children. They may also have to manage comments or even criticism of their parenting skills, made by family or unthinking friends. This might make them additionally sensitive to any inferred criticism from a setting and so it is doubly important that you can be seen as an ally rather than another critic. Johari's window

(Luft & Ingham, 1955) is a useful way to remember the gaps we may have in our understanding of other people's lives. It demonstrates how different pieces in the jigsaw of information may or may not be available to us and how that can affect our understanding. The model is as in Figure 3.2 and an example can be seen that illustrates how misunderstandings can take place when limited information is available to parties.

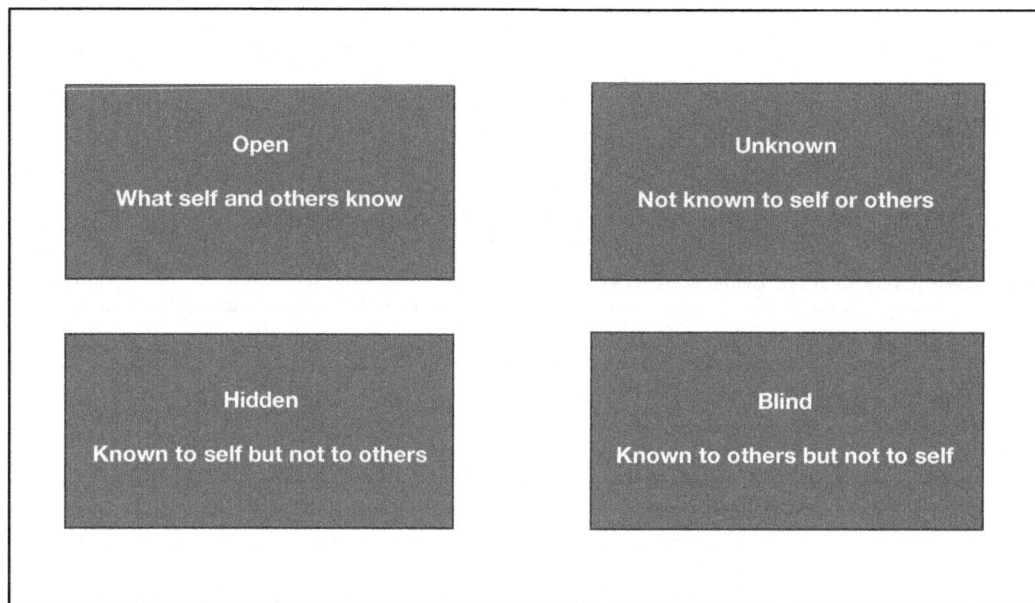

FIGURE 3.2 Johari window

Source: adapted from Luft & Ingham, *The Johari Window*, 1955.

What you both know (Open)

You both know that Jamie's mum collected him late three times in the past fortnight.

What neither of you know (Unknown)

That Jamie is about to develop an infection that will mean him staying at home for a week.

What you know and Jamie's mum doesn't (Hidden)

That you are studying for a Foundation Degree and you have an assignment due in next week. As a full time practitioner, every minute at home studying makes a difference.

What Jamie's mum knows and you don't (Blind)

That her mother has just had a cancer diagnosis and so Jamie's mum has the worry of her mum's illness plus the loss of her childcare support.

It is possible to see that the gaps in knowledge and information contained in this story could lead to tensions and possible misunderstanding, because both practitioner and parent had pressures on them that could easily lead them to focus on their own problems. Had there been more open information, a greater understanding of the challenges in their lives could have built tolerance and empathy.

Here is another activity to help you reflect upon how you can get to know parents better.

⚡ Short activity: Intercultural sensitivity

How do you demonstrate your awareness and understanding of the different cultural groups that visit your setting on a daily basis? Discuss as a group how the setting demonstrates intercultural sensitivity (Table 3.6).

TABLE 3.6 Intercultural sensitivity: activity

• Cultural representation in the staff
• Language displays where parents can see
• Leaflets in relevant languages
• Other?
• Action plan?

Using strengths-based practice

Strengths-based practice is a model of working with parents that is aspirational, positive, avoids judgements and emphasises hope, trust and positive expectations for the parents.

A strengths-based approach:

- is when helpers place a positive emphasis on resilience and protective factors, assets and strengths;
- establishes expectations for success within an individual's capacities;

- sets in motion forces for improvement;
- assumes that all families want good outcomes for the children and will use whatever is available to them to achieve that goal.

A strengths-based approach also:

- requires practitioners to recognise protective and resilience factors as well as risks;
- assumes that all families want good outcomes for the children and will use whatever is available to them to achieve that goal. (CWDC, 2010)

This approach can take some practice and sometimes a cultural change within a setting is required. It is understood that when a parent has been consistently unengaged, possibly unreliable and reluctant to participate in events or meetings that you have organised, it can be challenging to take a strengths-based approach initially. However, it can be achieved with practice and with a strong lead from the management of the setting. The listening skills that you are using can be developed with a 'strengths-based' focus in mind.

Strategies for managers

A range of reviews on effective strategies for managers to lead on and develop within their settings are identified below. Here they summarise the successful aspects of successfully implementing change in a setting:

- top down leadership, planning for whole school approach;
- sensitive collaboration and engagement;
- staff training;
- flexibility: ability to adapt strategies for engagement with the parents' needs;
- outward facing, two-way strategy;
- leaders with clear vision and values.

(Goodall & Vorhaus, 2011)

- identification of collective vision;
- shared understandings, meanings and goals;
- capacity to influence others into action;
- routine review of current practice and policy (contextualisation);
- effective communication/encouraging parent partnerships;
- reflection on practice/monitoring and assessing practice;
- ongoing professional development/learning community/team culture;
- distributed leadership.

(Siraj-Blatchford & Manni, 2006)

Longer activity: Activity for managers/room leaders

- in your senior management team, agree a priority that you would like to consider;
- develop three steps towards increasing parental engagement, mapping against some of the strategies above;
- justify your approach, anticipating the challenges that may affect your planning;
- make it parent-centred.

This chapter has covered many of the essential issues that challenge practitioners in their relationships with some parents. Hopefully it will have given your team an opportunity to think in depth about the ways that barriers and blocks to communication can be slowly dismantled (Table 3.7).

TABLE 3.7 Practice review

Chapter section	Fully engaged with strategies in place	Somewhat engaged	Further development needed
Identifying barriers			
Listening to parents			
Strengths-based practice			
Reflection on chapter			
What changes have you made?			
What needs further development?			

References

Blackmore, J. & Hutchison, K. (2010). Ambivalent relations: the 'tricky footwork' of parental involvement in school communities. *International Journal of Inclusive Education, 14* (5), 499–515.

Brooker, L. (2010). Constructing the triangle of care: Power and professionalism in practitioner/parent relationships. *British Journal of Educational Studies, 58* (2), 181–196.

Byrd, R. (2012). Conducting successful home visits in multicultural communities. *Journal of Curriculum and Instruction, 6* (1), 43–54. www.joci.ecu.edu/index.php/JoCI/article/view/128/PDF

Children's Workforce Development Council (CWDC). (2010). *Families going forward learner. Resources.* Online: http://webarchive.nationalarchives.gov.uk/20130616025318/ https://www.education.gov.uk/a00203696//childrenandyoungpeople/families/a00203696/ families-going-forward

Department for Education (DfE) (2017). *Statutory framework for the early years foundation stage.* London: DfE.

Goodall, J. & Vorhaus, J. (2011). *Review of best practice in parental engagement: Research Report DFE-RR156.* London: Department for Education.

Kohl, G.O., Langua, L.J. & McMahon, R.J. (2000) Parent involvement in school: Conceptualizing multiple dimensions and their relations with family and demographic risk factors. *Journal of School Psychology, 38* (6), 501–523. Online: www.ncbi.nlm.nih.gov/pmc/articles/ PMC2847291/pdf/nihms-148599.pdf

Kremer-Sadlik, T. & Fatigante, M. (2015). Investing in children's future: Cross-cultural perspectives and ideologies on parental involvement in education. *Childhood, 22* (1), 67–84.

Luft, J. & Ingham, H. (1955). The Johari window, a graphic model of interpersonal awareness. *Proceedings of the western training laboratory in group development.* Los Angeles, CA: UCLA.

National College for Teaching and Leadership (NCTL) (2013). *Teachers' standards (early years).* Retrieved from: https://www.gov.uk/government/uploads/system/uploads/attachment_data/file/ 211646/Early_Years_Teachers__Standards.pdf

Office for Standards in Education (Ofsted) (2018). *Early years inspection handbook.* London: Ofsted.

Siraj-Blatchford, I. & Manni, L. (2006). *Effective leadership in the early years sector (ELEYS).* London: University of London.

Whitmarsh, J. (2011). Othered voices: asylum-seeking mothers and early years education. *European Early Childhood Research Journal, 19* (4), 535–551. https://doi.org/10.1080/1350293X.2011.623540

4 The beginning of your transformation

Parental engagement in your setting

TABLE 4.1 Links to EY documentation

Teachers' Standards (Early Years), (NCTL, 2013)	Early years inspection handbook (Ofsted, updated 2018)	*Statutory framework for early years foundation stage (DfE, 2017)*
1.1 2.7 4.3 8.1	s. 80 (p. 17)	

While looking at the legal requirements of early years settings in Chapter 2, it is clear that the dominant feature in terms of information sharing and exchange is the relationship between parent and practitioner. Whether it is called partnership with parents, parental engagement or parental involvement, its defining success criteria are the relationships that evolve between families and settings.

This chapter introduces the process of the setting review, considering the question: *Where are you now?* Here there are opportunities for reflection and activities for the leadership team as well as practitioners to consider the ways they engage with parents; the extent to which parents' voices are heard in decisions made in the setting; reflective activities on setting practice; individual and team activities to look at staff practice and existing skills.

By identifying the starting point of *Where are you now?*, staff in your setting can set targets, manage expectations, share developmental ideas and, by the time you reach the review chapter at the end of the manual, celebrate progress.

This chapter looks at aspects of partnership working, parental engagement (PE) and parental involvement (PI) from the dual perspectives of leadership and practitioner involvement. Activities allow for reflection and discussion for management, practitioners and parents (Table 4.2), based on

- Leading transformation
- Partnership with parents
- Target setting
- Developing a vision

TABLE 4.2 Practice reflection

Chapter section	Fully engaged with strategies in place	Somewhat engaged	Further development needed
Strong leadership and strategies for partnership			
Partnership with parents			
Target setting for increased parental involvement			
Developing a vision that is clear to all: parents, practitioners and children.			
What strategies are currently in place?			
What needs further development?			

Overnight reflection

Reflect on the term *Where are we now* from your perspective, in relation to working in partnership with parents.

Leading transformation

The role of the leader is very important as team leaders have to motivate, empathise, prioritise and create a safe environment for staff and parents, highlighting the importance of understanding the complex issues surrounding partnership work, judgemental practitioners; sensitive communication skills; recognising safeguarding and confidentiality issues and managing them (Table 4.3). Taking responsibility for training staff is a fundamental element of leadership.

Longer activity: Leadership

Taking these points created by Goodall & Vorhaus (2010), discuss and consider the strengths and areas for development within the setting:

TABLE 4.3 Leadership: activity

	Strengths	Developmental areas
Top down leadership, planning for whole school approach		
Sensitive collaboration and engagement		
Staff training		
Flexibility: ability to adapt strategies for engagement with the parents' needs		
Outward facing, two-way strategy		
Leaders with clear vision and values		

Longer activity: Activity for senior managers and room leaders

Successful leadership of an early years setting requires the use of the skills on the left-hand side of Table 4.3 in order to ensure consistency and coherence in a setting.

Look at the categories on the left-hand side of Table 4.3. Reflecting on those skills, work with a partner to consider your present position in relation to barriers, relationships, wider family and information sharing (or anything else you want to add).

Divide a sheet of paper up into the leadership headings in Table 4.4, left, in order to share your views on how far you are developing with your visions and strategies. You can add different topics into the mix and different aspects of parental involvement, but try to keep the headings on the left to help you to reflect on the way you work as a team. Agree three or four key findings and add them at the bottom. These will help you to reflect on *Where we are now*.

TABLE 4.4 Skills for successful leadership: activity

Leadership skills	Aspects of parental involvement
Sharing a vision	Barriers
Developing strategies	Relationship between parents and practitioners
Ability to reflect	Widening links with the whole family
Ability to engage whole team responsiveness to needs and ideas from staff or parents	Information sharing
Key findings	

Once you have done this you will start to develop a picture of what the management feel are the issues. The next step is to see how practitioners and parents feel, so now move on to the next set of exercises for staff.

Training opportunities

> To engage effectively with parents, staff require training and coaching, particularly when working with parents whose backgrounds are very different to their own. School staff should therefore receive parental engagement training through initial teacher training or continuing professional development.
>
> (Goodall & Vorhaus, 2010, p. 7)

Regular staff training is important, even when funding is limited. It means that your staff have access to the most recent information and guidance on best practice, and it also means that you are investing in them. If you do not already have this in one place, build a staff record of who has completed what training, to help you maintain regular inputs to improve practice regularly in your setting.

Leaders should keep a record of training sessions to demonstrate their commitment to staff training (Table 4.5).

TABLE 4.5 Staff training: Activity

Name and role of practitioner	Event and notes	Date
E.g. Josh Parry, room leader and key person.	Staff meeting on listening to parents. To be repeated every two years. Used Wilson manual.	4/05/2018

Working in partnership with parents

What does the research say about partnership with parents?

Staff at the setting will benefit from an understanding of the research that shows that parental involvement is good for children's wellbeing. You could put this message into the staff room or somewhere that staff – and parents – will see how your setting prioritises work done with parents.

> The most important finding from the point of view of this review is that parental involvement in the form of 'at home good parenting' has a significant positive effect on children's achievement and adjustment even after all other factors shaping attainment have been taken out of the equation . . . The scale of the impact is evident across all social classes and all ethnic groups.
>
> (Desforges & Abouchaar, 2003, p. 5)
>
> Recent research has shown the impact of parental warmth, stability, consistency and boundary setting in helping children develop . . . skills.
>
> (DfES, 2007, p. 5)
>
> The concept of partnership may not be so readily transferable outside a western context . . .
>
> (Whitmarsh, 2011, p. 538)
>
> One of the most important findings in this literature is that parents' decisions about involvement are influenced by schools. Specifically, the research suggests that schools may take steps to enhance parents' active role construction and sense of efficacy for helping children learn; enact practices that support school, teacher, and student invitations to involvement; and adapt involvement requests and suggestions to the circumstances of parents' life contexts.
>
> (Hoover-Dempsey et al., 2005, p. 123)

This section is for all staff, so you might want to start here with an ice-breaking activity, or just ask them to discuss their overnight reflection and to start thinking about working with parents as partners. Then you can move into the next activities.

Longer activity: Working in partnership with parents

Most settings use a range of strategies to maintain positive relationships with the parents who bring their children to the setting. The use of a range of communications methods can assist in developing these relationships, giving parents choices in the way that they access information from the setting.

Epstein identified a typology of forms of involvement that spanned from the offering of parental support to being a part of the governing body. Use them in a staff activity to identify what your setting is doing in terms of a range of different activities (Table 4.6).

TABLE 4.6 Epstein's typology (2002): activity

Epstein's typology of parental engagement (2002)	My setting does this in these ways	Positives	Negatives
Parenting (supporting families and parent education)			
Communicating (effective home–school and school–home communications)			
Volunteering (recruiting help and support from parents)			
Learning at home (info to parents re learning)			
Decision making (including parents as participants through governance, committees)			
Collaborating with the community (integrating resources from community (businesses/other schools/civic awareness)			

How does the engagement in your setting measure against Epstein's typology (2002)? There are other typologies that overlap and that are more contemporary, for example Table 4.7. You can choose the one that seems to have the best fit with your setting.

Longer activity: Parental involvement

TABLE 4.7 Parental involvement according to Desforges & Abouchaar (2003): activity

	My setting does this in these ways	Positives	Negatives
Good parenting in the home			
Intellectual stimulation			
Parent–child discussion			
Good models of constructive social and educational values and high aspirations relating to personal fulfilment and good citizenship			
Contact with schools to share information			
Participation in school events			
Participation in the work of the school			
Participation in school governance			

You can see from Tables 4.6 and 4.7 that one links closely to activities that are led by the setting, and the other focuses more on things that parents may be doing to engage in their child's education but that don't automatically involve the school.

Completing one or both of these activities will help you and the team to see that some activities may work better than others in your setting and you may find that the reason one of your 'wishes', from the earlier activity, has not taken place is because there are some barriers to making it work. No matter. At this stage, the important thing is to see what exactly is going on. But do bear in mind the following and share the headline with staff:

Just because you do not see a parent often doesn't mean that they are not engaged

There are clear expectations about working in partnership with parents through EYFS. Within this document, the importance of working in partnership is emphasised but this is something that cannot be assumed and a number of literature reviews point out the difficulties of proving what impact different interventions might have (Gorard & See, 2013). They are a multitude of reasons why a parent may not be visible in a setting. The least likely explanation is that they do not care.

Exploring parental engagement and parental involvement – one, other or both?

There are many phrases in common currency across early years and primary settings – they all revolve around the principle of partnerships with parents and the use of methods and strategies that are implemented in order to encourage participation and also to demonstrate the ways in which the parents' voices can be heard within a setting (this is something that Ofsted are keen to hear about).

Longer activity: Parental engagement or involvement?

It is argued that there are differences between the meaning of the terms 'parental engagement' and 'parental involvement' (Goodall & Montgomery, 2014; Table 4.8). What do you think are the differences between engagement and involvement? In groups, come up with five examples of engagement, five examples of involvement. Then look at your examples and develop a definition of each of them – what is the fundamental difference? Is it just a matter of semantics or does it really mean different things?

TABLE 4.8 Engagement, involvement: what's the difference? activity

Engagement, involvement, what's the difference?				
Engagement	Engagement	Engagement	Engagement	Engagement
Involvement	Involvement	Involvement	Involvement	Involvement

Once you have started talking about your understandings of PI and PE, use the captions in Table 4.9 (you could cut them out and laminate them) – fit them into one or other of the categories in Table 4.8. Then discuss why you have chosen which.

TABLE 4.9 Engagement/involvement: activity

Where do these fit?				
A parent reading with their child at home	A parent reading with children in the setting	Organising fundraising for the setting	A parent talking to their child about show and tell	A parent arranging to see their child's key person
A parent completing the 'All about me' form	A parent telling you about their child's medication requirements	A parent agreeing to a home visit	A parent who is a teacher giving detailed information on what their child's developmental needs are	A parent talking to their child about the importance of learning

The answer is that all of these are examples of parental engagement OR involvement and it really doesn't matter which term you use, but if you can come to an agreement within the setting of what is more effective in terms of working with parents, then this activity will have worked for you.

Some of them might be less visible and some might be more challenging for practitioners but they all have some element of valuing education so that their child is able to see the importance of learning. You may not be able to see these quiet moments going on, but that is not to say that they do not exist so always assume that they are going on.

You are more likely to hear about them by demonstrating your respect and value of parents when you see them, assuming that they are already engaged in the education of their child.

Longer activity: Direction of travel

Think about the ways that we share information. Draw large arrows on a piece of flip chart paper and, in groups, share thoughts about the information that travels from setting to parent, then from parent to setting (Figure 4.1). How do they compare? How much do you hear from the parents and could you use more information travelling in one direction or the other? In our busy settings, there is a constant exchange of information, as we ensure that parents have the information from us that they need. But do we have enough from them? Is your information exchange a one-way or a two-way street? Use the diagram in Figure 4.1 to find out more:

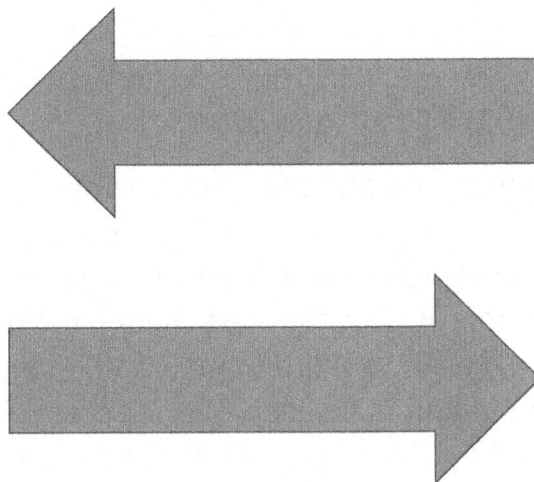

FIGURE 4.1 Information transfer – which direction?

CASE STUDY

Gita and Vlad have been bringing their son Marek to nursery for two years now. Marek is two and a half. The family have been living in the UK for three years, and both parents work full-time. When they first came to the nursery, Gita took responsibility for dropping off and collecting and spoke little English. She did not want to get involved because her English was

continued

limited and she did not know what was expected. It was much easier to let the 'experts' get on with the job of looking after her children. Neither she nor Vlad believed that pre-school nurseries did more than provide a childcare service. She did not feel that she needed to engage with the setting but was never rude to them.

It was hard for Gita to get to know the staff at the nursery because for a year, there was a high staff turnover. That and the added complication of not speaking much English meant that she avoided situations where she would have to repeat the things that she had already told one member of staff. Nobody seemed particularly friendly anyway, and she felt that the other mothers were keeping a wide berth and that they were staring at her when she came and went – there was a group of them who were always laughing and joking with the staff. She was afraid they would say something that she would not understand, so she avoided any engagement.

Of course, she and Vlad always read to the children before they went to bed, and they talked to them about the world around them when they went out for walks. No TV until they're older, they'd agreed, because they knew how important it was to give their kids a good start.

One day when Gita went to the nursery, someone she did not recognise greeted her in Polish – it was a new manager who wanted to welcome all parents in their own language! At first Gita was sceptical – it was only one word – and told Vlad about it. But the next thing Gita knew, there were leaflets in different languages in the entrance hall – so you could find out what the children were learning. This all took Vlad and Gita by surprise, especially as they found out how much their children were learning through play and how this would help them start school.

Over the next six months, the new key person in the nursery (who has stayed the longest of all) took the trouble to find out more about the family. When he found out that Vlad was a paramedic and Gita a care worker, he asked them to come and talk to the children about their jobs

It has taken a long time and some misunderstanding for the family to feel that they belong in the setting. Gita realised that she felt left out when she saw the other parents talking and accepted that it was mainly her anxiety that made her avoid these situations. As she got to know the key person, she was able to share her anxieties. He then helped her to get to know other parents.

- **What else could be done to make the process of including a family in the life of the setting quicker and more effective?**

- **Could any of Gita's anxieties been pre-empted?**

Longer activity: Questionnaire

In order to see *where you are now*, a reliable method is the use of a survey, or questionnaire. See the section below, which explains the importance of getting consent to collect data before you start.

This is an activity that will take you a little longer – certainly, days, possibly weeks, maybe even months. However, it is an opportunity to gather some rich data about the families in your setting. You could discuss it in one of your staff meetings. Perhaps one of your staff members is completing an early years qualification (Foundation Degree, BA, Early Years Teacher Status) and would be able to use this in their studies. Here are some suggested questions, but you could add more. A useful exercise would be to see how the results from the parents compare with the results of the practitioners. On the next page, you will find some ideas for a poster that you can pin up on a noticeboard. You might also want to translate it for those for whom English is not their first language.

Important preparation for your survey

You must conform to ethical guidelines when you are gathering information from people, especially in terms of confidentiality and usage. You should prepare a handout for potential participants letting them know:

- the purpose of the information;
- whether it will be anonymous;
- who will see what participants write;
- how it will be stored;
- when it will be destroyed.

You may not use it for any other purpose. You could even add this information to the survey so participants can see it as they complete it.

You can find out more here:

www.smartsurvey.co.uk/articles/gdpr-compliant-with-data-collection

This new legislation came in during May 2018 and relates to data protection.

For parents and for practitioners – do your own action research

TABLE 4.10 Practitioner survey

Practitioners
Choose an answer that describes your role: • Manager • Deputy • Key person • Room leader • Practitioner • SENCO • Other?
What age children are you working with?
What does 'working in partnership with parents' mean to you? Please answer in your own words
What words would you use to describe your experience of partnership with parents – use as many as you like.
Can you give any examples of when 'partnership with parents' has worked effectively?
Can you give any examples of when it has not worked effectively?
What are the factors that challenge 'partnerships with parents'?
What would you suggest to improve partnership work?
What do you think makes a setting feel 'parent-friendly'?

TABLE 4.11 Parent survey

Parents
How old are your children?
What does 'working in partnership with parents' mean to you? Please answer in your own words
What words would you use to describe your experience of partnership with parents – use as many as you like
Can you give any examples of when 'partnership with parents' has worked effectively?
Can you give any examples of when it has not worked effectively?
What are the factors that challenge 'partnerships with parents'?
What would you suggest to improve partnership work?
What do you think makes a setting feel 'parent-friendly'?

This is short and simple – but can generate many ideas and it can be interesting to see the differences or similarities between the views of parents and practitioners (Tables 4.10, 4.11). Once participants have completed the questionnaire, you can analyse the information, and find out what is important to them. This is a way of listening to both parents and practitioners, seeing how much their perceptions overlap and whether there are 'quick fix' opportunities to improve practice.

Poster

PARENTS!

WE WANT YOUR VIEWS!

★ **Please take a questionnaire**

★ **Complete and return**

★ **Word version available too!**

★ **Let us know what you think about some important parts of our work together.**

★ **Talk to**

_____

for more information

So as we move towards the end of this chapter, there may be many areas that you want to think about. Here are a couple of activities that you can use to develop some targets and to discuss the ways that you will approach these issues. This chapter has focused on where you are now in the setting, looking at the meaning of partnership and encouraging you to identify what you are doing to listen to parents regularly. It only remains for you: practitioners, parents and children, to work on a vision for the setting in terms of goals and objectives.

Target setting for increasing parental engagement

Longer activity: Target setting

This activity can be developed from the findings of any research that you do, or you can choose some areas that you want to make a priority in the development of your setting's practice (Table 4.12).

For managers and room leaders

- in pairs, agree a priority that you would both like to consider;
- develop three steps towards increasing parental engagement, mapping against some of the evidence from previous discussions;
- justify your approach, anticipating the challenges that may affect your planning;
- make it parent-centred by considering change through a parent's viewpoint and try to maximise advantages for the parent.

Developing a vision which is clear to all: parents, practitioners and children

Poster

This time, you will design the poster. You should involve everyone in it, should they choose to be involved. Use the findings from the survey to inform the poster, sharing information with parents about the findings and inviting them to get creative. You could either go online to find software and apps that will 'scramble' your words into a design or you can be as creative as you have time for.

Your target is to create a clear and attainable, shared vision (Table 4.13).

Table 4.12 Target setting: activity

TARGET	Three steps	Rationale and challenges	Parent-centred – how?
Engaging with wider family	1 start with room xxx	This fits in with our trust-building targets and the children will love it.

Challenge: time | Will widen family support |
	2 talk to parents for views		A conversation starter with children to share between home and setting
	3 plan an Open Day		Will base on initial feedback
	1		
	2		
	3		
	1		
	2		
	3		
	1		
	2		
	3		
	1		
	2		
	3		

TABLE 4.13 Practice review

Chapter section	Fully engaged with strategies in place	Somewhat engaged	Further development needed
Strong leadership and strategies for partnership			
Developing partnership with parents			
Target setting for increased parental involvement			
Developing a vision, which is clear to all: parents, practitioners and children.			
Reflection on chapter			
What changes have you made?			
What needs further development?			

References

Department for Education and Skills. (2007). *Every parent matters*. Nottingham: DfES.

Department for Education (DfE) (2017). *Statutory framework for the early years foundation stage*. London: DfE.

Desforges, C. & Abouchaar, A (2003). *The impact of parental involvement, parental support and family education on pupil achievement and adjustment: a review of literature*. Nottingham: DfES.

Epstein, J.L., Sanders, M.G., Simon, B.S., Salinas, K.C., Jansom, N.R. & Voorhis, F.L. (2002). *School, family and community partnerships: Your handbook for action* (2nd ed.) CA: Corwin. Available at: www.csos.jhu.edu/p2000/nnps_model/school/sixtypes/6types.htm

Goodall, J. & Montgomery, C. (2014). Parental involvement to parental engagement: a continuum. *Educational Review*, 66 (4), 399–410.

Goodall, J. & Vorhaus, J. (2010). *Review of best practice in parental engagement*. DfE RR 156. London: DfE.

Gorard, S. & See, B.H. (2013). *Do parental involvement interventions increase attainment? A review of the evidence*. London: Nuffield Foundation.

Hoover Dempsey, K. V., Walker, J. M. T., Sandler, H.M., Whetsel, D., Green, C.L., Wilkins, A.S. & Closson, K. (2005). Why Do Parents Become Involved? Research Findings and Implications. *The Elementary School Journal*, 106 (2), 105–130.

National College for Teaching and Leadership (NCTL) (2013). *Teachers' standards (early years)*. Retrieved from: https://www.gov.uk/government/uploads/system/uploads/attachment_data/file/211646/Early_Years_Teachers__Standards.pdf

Office for Standards in Education (Ofsted) (2018). *Early years inspection handbook*. London: Ofsted.

Whitmarsh, J. (2011). Othered voices: Asylum-seeking mothers and early years education. *European Early Childhood Education Research Journal*, 19 (4), 535–551

5 | Supporting transitions
Helping children and families adapt to change

TABLE 5.1 Links to EY documentation

Teachers' Standards (Early Years), (NCTL, 2013)	Early years inspection handbook (Ofsted, updated 2018)	*Statutory framework for early years foundation stage (DfE, 2017)*
2.3 5.1 5.4 8.3	s. 153 (p. 33) s. 156 (p. 36 and p. 37) s. 157 (p. 38)	s. 1.7 (p. 9) s. 1.10 (p. 10) s. 3.27 (p. 22) s. 3.47 (p. 28) s. 3.72 (p. 32)

Transitions are a cultural construct – understanding the expectations of families will help your role. Who gets involved in transitions (mothers, fathers, wider family) reflects changing cultural expectations of childhood and roles (Vogler *et al.*, 2008).

This chapter will explore the ways in which you can apply best practice to the process of managing change for children and their parents. You will find activities that will increase understanding of the range of transitions that we all experience, and reflect upon the ways that they can be managed, including home visits and movements between rooms. The chapter will also give you opportunities to review current practice and update or develop your transitions policy.

Before starting the chapter, reflect on the content in Table 5.2.

- Understanding transitions
- Reflecting on transitions
- Preparing for transitions
- Home visits
- Transition policy

Understanding transitions

TABLE 5.2 Practice reflection

Chapter section	Fully engaged with strategies in place	Somewhat engaged	Further development needed
Understanding transitions			
Reflecting on your own experiences of transitions			
Preparing for transitions			
Home visits			
Reviewing or developing a transition policy			
What strategies are currently in place?			
What needs further development?			

Overnight reflection

Think about a transition that you have made, perhaps starting a new school or a new job.

● What were the feelings that went through you mind in the week leading up to the change?
● What were the causes of those feelings?
● Did that have an impact on your behaviour?
● What could you transfer from that experience when you plan for transitions for children now?

Transitions

There are a number of types of transition, all of which require adaptation by children and their families in terms of expectation and understanding of new routines. Kagan and Neuman (1998) write about vertical and horizontal transitions:

Vertical – educational or social (rites of passage, once and for all). For a child, the move from home to setting is likely to be the most significant vertical transition in a child's life at that point, with new buildings, routines, people, food, smells, etc. to manage. Others can include:

- moving from milk only to solid diet;
- moving out of nappies;
- cutting first teeth;
- sleeping through the night;
- developmental transitions such as crawling, walking.

Horizontal – movements between various spheres of a child's life (home to school, school to caregiver, daily transitions) – also referred to as 'border crossings' (Kagan & Neuman 1998, p. 336).

These transitions are less significant in terms of scale, but they require a child to make adaptations on a regular basis.

QUOTE FOR DISCUSSION OR REFLECTION

Horizontal transitions are less distinctive than vertical transitions and occur on an everyday basis. They refer to the movements children (or indeed any human being) routinely make between various spheres or domains of their lives (e.g., everyday movements between home and school or from one caretaking setting to another). These structure children's movement across space and over time, and into and out of the institutions that impact on their well-being.

(Vogler *et al.*, 2008, p. 2)

Discuss possible opportunities and challenges for practitioners and leaders in managing smaller transitions

---

Children undergo a series of transitions even before they start school, and managing them effectively can lead to increased security and confidence, as they develop trust in the people around them that they will be emotionally supported during times of change and uncertainty. Children who feel prepared and supported for a transition are more likely to be able to process the situation emotionally, whereas a transition that is presented to a child without due preparation may result in anxiety, potentially setting a negative model and a possible resistance to change in the future. The transitions that a child will experience will also have a significant effect on parents, so the more you can involve them in the planning; the more positive the experience will be for all involved.

One significant transition is the move from pre-school to school (you will find more information about this in Chapter 8), but it is worth noting that:

> *While school commencement is undoubtedly amongst the most significant milestones in early childhood, the transitions leading up to this point are less well understood. In particular, the transitions that occur within early childhood care and education (ECCE) settings, as children progress from one age group and room to another, have been relatively overlooked. As a result there is a considerable gap in knowledge concerning how best to promote positive moves for children and their families during these early transitions.*
>
> (O'Farrelly & Hennessy, 2014, pp. 329–330)

The transition from one level of education to the next may involve a requirement for the child to be more independent, and one parent felt that this increased independence had a negative impact on the welcome that parents felt in the new environment:

> *nobody is looking to shoo you out of the room, but you are a lot more conscious of it than I ever was in the (pre-transition) room . . . definitely it's a case of drop and out you go.*
>
> (O'Farrelly & Hennessy, 2014, p. 338)

As practitioners, you may have some understanding of how this can happen, especially in the move from pre-school to reception class. The next section will ask practitioners to explore their own experiences of transitions, not necessarily those that take place in the setting.

QUOTES FOR DISCUSSION OR REFLECTION

Compare this first quote:

> *Gender differences were apparent in parents' reports. Specifically, parents of daughters tended to refer to assertive and independent behaviours: 'she is more assertive and more independent . . . and I suppose isn't just a shrinking violet'. Conversely, parents of boys described more marked and negative changes in their sons, such as instances of aggression: 'it was the first time he ever bit'; temper tantrums.*
>
> (O'Farrelly & Hennessy, 2014, p. 355)

With this second one:

> *Transition is a part of life that we all deal with in our own ways. How we deal with it largely depends on our early experiences of transitions and how these were dealt with.*
>
> (McCarthy, 2013, np)

To what extent do you agree with these quotes? Is our ability to manage transitions based on our early experiences or on our personality, including gender identity?

Reflecting on your own experience of transitions

We have all been through a range of transitions, and there are a number of cultural stages that we go through, reflecting importance milestones in our lives. These could include religious ceremonies marking birth, marriage and death, as well as educational milestones, and physical stages of development that bring with them changes and adjustments from one condition to the next.

Longer activity: Transitions in society

Think of transitions that fit in each of the categories in Table 5.3.

All of these transitions indicate a move to another life stage, with the attendant changed expectations, for example, when puberty arrives, there is an expectation to manage the physical and emotional changes that take place for adolescents. This can be challenging

TABLE 5.3 Transitions in society: activity

• **Social and cultural**   (e.g. Christening, Bah Mitvzah)
• **Gender specific**   (e.g. coming of age ceremonies, hen or stag events as part of the transition to married status)
• **Educational**   (e.g. moving from KS1 to KS2)
• **Human development**   (e.g. puberty, learning how to walk)

during the period immediately surrounding the transition phase, which is why it is so important to plan carefully for transitions, especially for younger children.

In the next activity, we shall be considering transitions in the setting, and how parents have been involved.

Short activity

Reflect upon the ways that you have worked in partnership with parents in order to support transitions.

Having thought about your own experiences of transitions in the overnight reflection, share some of your reflections with the team and complete the following:

Transitions

The most important thing to remember about transitions is:

Share these with the group – are there many different ideas? How would you prioritise these? All the same level of importance or can you put them on a scale? They will all be important to somebody and based on their own experiences so there is no right or wrong – don't discard any ideas – they all have a value so be sensitive.

Preparation for transitions

Use Table 5.4 (p. 78) to reflect on what the change is and how children can be prepared, drawing in resources from families. Sometimes (often?) parents find a change as challenging as children, so reflect on how you share information with them in order to maintain open lines of communication. You will find a blank version of this table in the downloadable resources.

Transitions can hold both new opportunities and unknown worries. A child may be unsure of who they will be friends with when they move to a new room. They become a small fish in a new and unknown pond, whereas before they had the status of being one of the experienced children in the room. In the next room, they could be the youngest and the least familiar with the structure, the people, everything (O'Farrelly & Hennessy, 2014, p. 342).

Transition can be supported by the following:

- preparation
- familiarisation
- listening
- sharing information.

Table 5.5 is another activity template that you can use to map against a child's development. The activity can be chosen to reflect the child's developmental stage, and completing this will give you opportunities to share ideas and planning with parents.

Longer activity: Transitions

See Table 5.5 (p. 79).

TABLE 5.4 Preparation for transitions: activity

Name of transition: E.g. *room transfer*	Description of what is in place	Action/date
What is familiar in new stage?	*Same nursery; same building; new room which looks similar*	*Visit to room to look for new key person and meet*
Priming for change and preparing for change	*Visits planned*	*1.12.18*
Security (transition) object.	*Not in place*	*KP will bring something from the room for children to play with and bring back*
Key person – communication re transition and individual needs	*Meeting planned with KP, 1.12.18*	*Check actions from meeting have been implemented*
Children's sense of ownership, e.g. personal storage space	*Child's drawer in place.*	*Session to decorate drawer, bring something to put in drawer, 2.12.18*
Management of border crossings.		
Links and visits between local settings	*n/a*	
Communication with parents AND children about the process – ask parents and children how they like this to be managed.	*Meeting with parents and children to explain changes and ask for input*	*Parents suggested (a), and child agreed, so in place*
Role of parents – what information are you sharing with them? How can they support from home (books, talking to child etc.?)	*At meeting, felt that we needed a checklist*	*Actions discussed and agreed. We have given books to read at home but might want a checklist to be developed*
Timings		

RESOURCES **TABLE 5.5** Linking transitions to development: activity

Transitions activity		
What is the activity?		
What other developmental competencies can be evidenced in the activity?	1)	
	2)	
	3)	
Any barriers to the success of the activity? How can they be resolved?	Barriers	Resolutions

Home visits

> Home visits aim to allow parents and teachers and practitioners to get to know each other in familiar surroundings, whilst providing children with an opportunity to meet their teacher or key person.
>
> (Greenfield, 2011, p. 102)

Some settings organise a home visit for all new families. In general, the purpose of the home visit is to have the opportunity to meet the family in their own environment, where the family will feel most confident and the child be made to feel most relaxed. In this way, practitioners can make informal observations that will help them to prepare for their start at the settings. Practitioners find it helpful because the parents are often more open when in their own home and are prepared to share more information. They can start to build relationships with the family on a one-to-one basis. By bringing both setting information and one or two resources for the child to play with, they start to break down barriers and develop trusting relationships.

On the other hand, the home visit is not universally applied. There are disadvantages:

- It is labour intensive, ideally requiring two members of staff to be away from the setting.
- There are safety issues about going into unknown homes.
- Some parents find the visit patronising and judgemental.

However, these comments have been collected from a survey (Wilson, 2016, pp. 45–46) asking parents' and practitioners' for their views on home visits.

QUOTES FOR DISCUSSION OR REFLECTION

Comments from parents:

Home visits are more personal and parents/children are more relaxed. Parents are also likely to be given (a) chance to be more open with information regarding their child.

I like the fact that we had a home visit. It gave me the chance to discuss some private family issues so I felt happy Michael's home background was understood before he started.

It gave me a chance to discuss some private family issues so I felt happy that my child's background was understood before he started.

It is a very good opportunity to talk . . . because it happens in a familiar environment.

My son's nursery did a home visit – he loved it and I enjoyed the informal visit to our home.

Comments from practitioners

. . . offers the chance for a unique insight into the start of a wonderful partnership between nursery and home. A memorable event which can be key to supporting the child.

The value gained from home visiting is immense.

Excellent way to make parent and child feel at ease as they are on their own territory.

They make parents feel included and valued – give parents and children a chance to be seen in own setting and home territory – brilliant for minority groups, e.g. travellers, forces families etc.

Discuss the quotes above in small groups, in the context of the following questions:

- **What are the arguments for and against home visits?**

- **Is this something that you are doing already?**

- **Is it something that could work in your setting?**

- **Do you think you are gathering the rich data that you can get when you spend time alone with a family in other ways?**

Home visits

Although time consuming and labour intensive, a home visit can cement strong relationships and give practitioners an informative window into the world of the child and give families the space, territory and privacy to talk openly about their lives and children's needs. Visits are to be treated with sensitivity and training should be given to all practitioners who make home visits in order to assure quality, cultural sensitivity and safety.

CASE STUDY

Maria is a single parent with three children under four years. She is going back to work and her three-year-old will be starting at nursery next month. She lives in the local traveller community and when she approached the nursery and heard about the home visit, she felt very anxious about visitors to her home. The setting manager, Simran, stressed that she understood her feelings but also that it was part of the induction process and it would mainly benefit her son, Jamie. Simran asked whether there was a community centre where they could initially meet. Maria agreed to meet there and brought her family with her. The meeting went well because the practitioners were trained to work sensitively with her: they did not bring any forms with them, but Simran spent the time getting to know Jamie, while her colleague, Sam, spoke with Maria. After a little while, Maria felt more comfortable with the members of staff and they agreed to walk back to her home and continue there. This gave them a chance to let Jamie show them his room, which he shared with his siblings. He showed them his favourite toys, and the games that he liked to play. Maria was relieved that he was so comfortable with Sam and Simran, and when they brought some toys from the nursery, he became very interested in his visit which would be taking place in a couple of days.

At the end of the visit, Maria confided in them that she felt very wary about anyone looking around their home, because 'when the council people come round, they make judgments because I'm a traveller'. Sam and Simran assured her that this was not the intention; they just wanted to help Jamie get the most out of his time with them.

Later on, they found out that Maria was very self-conscious about her level of literacy, but they assured her that they could fill in the forms together. They feel that it would not have been possible to share these insecurities and elements of personal information in a setting visit.

Making the visit a success

There are many aspects to plan for when you set up home visits. More important than anything is to go to the visit with the intention of listening. Let parents and children talk to you about themselves. Few parents will be reluctant to talk about their children's achievements. This is an excellent opportunity to develop a trusting relationship, where you are sufficiently interested in them to visit them at home. It means that there will be familiar faces as they walk through the door; the child will be able to bring back a toy that you have left with them; a place will be prepared for them to leave their coat – already explained to them, as will other things so the family knows what to expect. You can leave some photos of the child's peg and drawer, where they will be playing, and so on. Some practitioners bring a story to read and leave the book with the child. You can makes notes when you leave – far more important is to go there uncluttered by any signs of officialdom, and sit with them. See Chapter 3 for more activities related to active listening.

What to bring with you

- information about the setting, which can be left with families – check it is in the correct language;
- photos of the setting;
- a translator, if the family do not have English as a first language;
- any relevant forms to complete when you have left, or while you are there if they prefer;
- something from the setting for the child, to be left with them;
- a colleague, as it is always better to visit in pairs;
- mobile phone.

Personal safety

As noted, personal safety is a factor and it is vital that all prospective visits are recorded, so someone knows where and when the visits are taking place. A code word and phone call can be planned in case of any threat. Although this may seem dramatic, it is important that all factors, risks and benefits are discussed and resolved before practitioners visit any home. You will find an activity relating to the development of a transition policy later in this chapter, but before you complete the 'home visit' section, you should be clear about how you plan these visits.

- Pets – one person's cuddly pet can be another's object of terror so do find out in advance. In addition, there may be some practitioners who are allergic to pets so ensure that you take any anti-allergen medication.
- Who might be there? – you may find that there are friends there, or that the TV is on all the time – be sensitive: the parent may be feeling very anxious and want some moral support – try to go with the flow, whatever it is, unless you feel uncomfortable.
- Seating – choose to sit on the floor, or nearest a door, until you have a good sense that you are safe.

- Accepting refreshments: this is a culturally sensitive area, so on the whole, just accept water, but if you feel it would be appropriate to accept other drinks, be guided by your research on the family culture that you are visiting.

Documentation

You will need to plan carefully for a home visit structure. There will be a need to carry out a risk assessment as part of your planning, in order to identify any potential risks and put steps into place to minimise the risk. You should also deliver training to members of staff who make home visits. You should use experienced members of staff as the lead practitioner for the visit and the structure of the visits should be agreed beforehand and shared during training. Issues such as length of visit, whether staff should accept hospitality (e.g. refreshments) should be clear beforehand. It should be clear how family information should be gathered, and what should be gathered.

QUOTES FOR DISCUSSION OR REFLECTION

Look at the quotations in Table 5.6 and consider your own experiences, then, reflect on the pros and cons of home visits.

TABLE 5.6 Home visits: activity

'The home visit is often the first contact a practitioner may have with a child and his or/her family and is a unique opportunity to lay the foundations for partnership with parents yet staff may not have received adequate training to enable them to utilize this opportunity.' (Greenfield, 2011, p. 102) 'It is not easy to knock on the door of a stranger, and even more difficult to begin to form a working relationship with that person. However, early years staff in this county are expected to do this: some do it very effectively, but others may not, and this could have a detrimental influence on the relationship between home and school.' (Greenfield, 2011, p. 102)
Pros of home visits
Cons of home visits:
Would you change anything about the way you carry out your home visits, having read this article?

Transition policy in your setting

The *Statutory Framework for the Early Years Foundation Stage* (DfE, 2017) does not require a setting to have a transition policy but it is good practice to have one so that all staff are aware of expectations and there is a consistency in practice across the setting.

Go online to find strong examples of transitions policies. Choose a sample of policies that reflect your type of setting. You will find that they may include information that:

- includes maps to the EYFS;
- includes the full range of transition events, from settling in visits, to room changes, to transition to school;
- shows how parents are included in transition arrangements;
- involves children as well as parents;
- shows how transition arrangements are organised;
- identifies effective transition practice;
- gives sample activities for a range of transitions, mapped to EYFS;
- demonstrates evidence of curriculum/framework continuity;
- gives examples of useful transition information.

Longer activity: Developing your policy

This activity could take a number of hours so it may be that you spend an hour gathering information from all staff, based on the questions in Table 5.7, and then work with a smaller project group.

Policy review

Preparation

Identify three or four sample policy documents from the internet and print them out, so that there is enough for one between three. Take your own policy and give a copy to each group of three.

Before handing out the policy samples, make decisions on the points raised in Table 5.7 (p. 87).

TABLE 5.7 Transition policy in your setting: activity

• What would I like to include in our policy that is not already there?
• What can we safely remove?
• How can we involve parents in the policy review?
• What do I want to learn from reading these policies?
• What would be useful for parents to know and how can we share this information with them?

Implementation

At the end of this chapter, you may review your transitions policy or develop it to include some revisions (Table 5.8). If you are planning on a revision, ensure that the sections included in this chapter are visible, and that you share it with parents for their views.

Further reading

Bulkeley, J. and Fabian, Dr H. (2006). Well-being and belonging during early educational transitions. *International Journal of Transitions in Childhood*, 2. Retrieved 15 January 2015 from https://extranet.education.unimelb.edu.au/LED/tec/pdf/journal2_bulkeley%20and%20 fabian.pdf

Fisher, J.A. (2009). 'We used to play in Foundation, it was more funner': Investigating feelings about transition from Foundation Stage to Year 1. *Early Years*, 29 (2), 131–145.

TABLE 5.8 Practice review

Chapter section	Fully engaged with strategies in place	Somewhat engaged	Further development needed
Understanding transitions			
Reflecting on your own experience of transitions			
Preparing for transitions			
Home visits			
Reviewing or developing a transition policy for the setting			
Reflection on chapter			
What changes have you made?			
What needs further development?			

Fisher, J. (2011). Building on the Early Years Foundation Stage: Developing good practice for transition into Key Stage 1. *Early Years, 31* (1), 31–42.

Kennedy, E., Cameron, R.J., & Greene, J. (2012). Transitions in the early years: Educational and child psychologists working to reduce the impact of school culture shock. *Educational & Child Psychology, 29* (1), 19–31.

Van Gennep, A. (1960). *The Rites of Passage*. Chicago, IL: University of Chicago Press.

Yeboah, D.A. (2002). Enhancing transition from early childhood phase to primary education: Evidence from the research literature. *Early Years, 22* (1), 51–68.

References

Department for Education (DfE) (2017). *Statutory framework for the early years foundation stage.* London: DfE.

Greenfield, S. (2011). Nursery home visits: Rhetoric and realities. *Journal of Early Childhood Research, 10* (1), 100–112. http://journals.sagepub.com/doi/pdf/10.1177/1476718X11407983

Kagan, S.L. & Neuman, M.J. (1998). Lessons from three decades of transition research. *The Elementary School Journal, 98* (4), 365–379.

McCarthy, A. (2013). *Transitions from Early Intervention Settings.* Available at: www.teaching expertise.com/articles/making-transitions-easier-2994

National College for Teaching and Leadership (NCTL) (2013). *Teachers' standards (early years).* Retrieved from: https://www.gov.uk/government/uploads/system/uploads/attachment_data/file/211646/Early_Years_Teachers__Standards.pdf

O'Farrelly, C. & Hennessy, E. (2014) Watching transitions unfold: a mixed-method study of transitions within early childhood care and education settings. *Early Years, 34* (4), 329–347.

Office for Standards in Education (Ofsted) (2018). *Early years inspection handbook.* London: Ofsted.

Vogler, P., Crivello, G. & Woodhead, M. (2008). *Early childhood transitions research: A review of concepts, theory, and practice.* Working Paper No. 48. The Hague, The Netherlands: Bernard van Leer Foundation. Retrieved 15 January 2015 from www.bernardvanleer.org/Early_childhood_transitions_research_A_review_of_concepts_theory_and_practice

Wilson, T. (2016). *Working with parents, carers and families in the early years: The essential guide.* Oxon: Routledge.

6 | Parental engagement in the baby room

TABLE 6.1 Links to EY documentation

Teachers' Standards (Early Years), (NCTL, 2013)	Early years inspection handbook (Ofsted, updated 2018)	*Statutory framework for early years foundation stage (DfE, 2017)*
2.2, 2.3	s. 157 (p. 38)	s. 1.10 (p. 10)

This chapter includes a guide to materials for signposting parents to local and national services. It will make use of current research to underpin ways of building a trusting relationship with new parents, the focus including:

- attachment and separation;
- sleep;
- finance and work issues;
- breastfeeding, traumatic birth and returning to work;
- postnatal depression.

There will be activities that increase understanding, to gather information from parents, to identify ways of involving new parents and their families in the setting.

Before you start this chapter, watch this, entitled *What every new parent should know*: www.youtube.com/watch?v=jskG0yVDMLk

This chapter focuses very explicitly on new parents, especially new mothers. This is because they have undergone so many physical and emotional changes since the birth of their child that it will help practitioners to reflect on the spectrum of transitions and adjustments that they have made, and then look like a human being as they walk out of their home and greet the rest of the world.

This is perhaps the easiest and the most challenging time to work with parents. Easy because parents are more likely to engage than at any other time, especially if this is their first baby. They may have been hunting for the best type of setting in which to leave their baby and will be soaking up information about the relative benefits and disadvantages of childminders, nurseries, nannies or using their own relatives. Most difficult because of the challenges they may be facing in terms of their physical and emotional health.

TABLE 6.2 Practice reflection

Chapter section	Fully engaged with strategies in place	Somewhat engaged	Further development needed
Trust building			
Attachment and separation			
Sleep and fatigue			
Work and finance			
Traumatic birth			
Supporting breastfeeding			
Postnatal depression			
What strategies are currently in place?			
What needs further development?			

It is not unusual for parents to be bombarded with well-intentioned advice from friends and family, but the visit to a nursery (and the home visit if you do these), will be an opportunity for parents to make decisions based on the evidence of the setting around them. The role of the setting is to inform but not sell, as this is an important and personal decision, one that will be based on context, relationships and individual preferences.

Trust building

Building trust may be easy or may be difficult but requires time, consistency and commitment. There are no sophisticated skills required to build trust, no expensive training courses. You can prove this to yourself by thinking about the people in your life that you trust. Why do you trust them? Because they have specific skills or because you can depend on them?

While it is easy to develop skills for a trusting relationship, it is also likely that new parents will be looking very closely and they will want to know that they are leaving their baby with practitioners they can trust.

Overnight reflection

Spend some time thinking about the people that you trust, and think why you trust them. Are they reliable? Do they understand you? Do they listen to you? What qualities do they have that help you to trust them? Bring your thoughts to the next training meeting.

Longer activity: What parents might be thinking

In the next activity, take a look at the thought clouds in Figure 6.1; these are just some of the feelings that parents might be coming to a setting with in the morning. Discuss how they might be feeling and whether there are other issues that might be facing them. You will also find a blank version of this as a downloadable resource – add your own feelings to it. You might be feeling angry that a parent has just been offhand towards you. With the use of this form and using discussion, think about how you can show parents that you understand what they might be undergoing and also manage your own feelings.

FIGURE 6.1 What parents might be thinking

Attachment and separation

The attachment relationship between a caregiver and infant is the way that infants instinctively ensure their survival through ensuring the strong bond between caregiver and infant (Bowlby, 1997; Howe, 2011). From the perspective of the parent, taking a child to nursery and entrusting them to relative strangers is an extreme act of faith. Whether you are a parent yourself or not, you will be able to understand the anxiety that some parents go through when they leave their children, especially when they are leaving first babies.

Many practitioners will understand that separating from their child can be painful for parents. Children are often distractible by playful activities when a parent leaves. Parents, on the other hand, have to contend with guilt and leaving a child who may be distressed. The ways that you help parents to manage this separation will help develop a trusting relationship between you and the parent. Your understanding and empathy may also help parents to regulate their feelings towards the child and their possible frustration and even anger at the child for making them feel so tired and stressed. For parents who have had little sleep and then need to go to work, a kind word and an expression of support can keep them going and demonstrate that someone understands how they may be feeling.

⚡ Short activity: Parent/child separation

Discuss the ways that you support a parent when they leave their child. What is most difficult for them? What is most difficult for you?

Use Table 6.3 to reflect on the challenges of the actual separation and to think of ways that you can demonstrate your understanding to parents.

Once you have completed Table 6.3, go back over the difficulties and agree the best ways to manage these situations. So, for example, look at the table, and add some further comments in a different colour pen, with possible solutions (see Table 6.4).

RESOURCES **TABLE 6.3** Parent/child separation: activity

Difficult for parents	Difficult for practitioners
Knowing the best moment to leave	Managing all children when one child is upset
Not wanting their child to feel rejected	Wanting the parent to leave to avoid dragging the separation out

TABLE 6.4 Parent/child separation: activity *2*

Difficult for parents	Difficult for practitioners
Knowing the best moment to leave Discuss during home or setting visit; assurance; no pressure to leave	Managing all children when one child is upset
Not wanting their child to feel rejected	Wanting the parent to leave to avoid dragging the separation out

Sleep

Many of the parents that will be dropping off their children to the baby room are likely to be sleep deprived. They may have had a series of broken nights and this may have been going on for many months. Research by van der Helm *et al.* (2010) suggests that this can also have a detrimental effect on the recognition of emotions, especially on the recognition of happy and angry faces. Poor infant sleep, leading to poor parental sleep, can also be an indicator for postnatal depression (Sadeh, Tikotzky & Scher, 2010). While there is little that you can do to improve a parent's sleep opportunities, it helps to understand what parents might be going through and perhaps give them some encouragement and reassurance that they are doing the right thing (Table 6.5).

Short activity: Role-playing

TABLE 6.5 Reflecting back: activity

One way you can show parents that you understand how they are feeling is by the way you talk to them, reflecting back what they are saying rather than dismissing it. Try responding to these comments in a supportive way, even when they are not easy. Once you have completed the first four, discuss what parents have said to you on bad days, and the best ways of responding. Talk also about how you feel when a parent is short with you and how you manage the situation.
E.g. Parent says: it's all right for you, playing all day!   You say: 'so it's a tough day for you today?'
Parent says: I'm just going to sneak out because I can't cope with a fuss this morning . . .   You say:
Parent says: I keep telling that friend of yours . . . no bottles!   You say:
Parent says: very little . . .   You say:

You can use the strategy of reflecting back what parents say, and also summarising or paraphrasing what you understand that they are saying, in many situations, not just when parents are tired. Practice it at home with your friends or family, and see how they respond to it! This practice emphasises the engagement of the listening, the value that the listener places upon the words that are being spoken to them, through active listening. By reflecting back to someone, or by paraphrasing ('so have I understood you right: you want to talk to the doctor about your worries?') you are giving that person space to express their thoughts and be listened to.

You may wonder why this is necessary, whether it is part of your job role, and you would be right to conclude that you should not take on anything that seems to feel like counselling or mentoring. These are strategies that can be used to build trust and help you to get to know the family better, which will help with your job in supporting the child in partnership with parents.

Work issues and finance

For parents, the years of raising a family are significantly more expensive than life as a single person or a couple. There may be a loss of income during the postnatal period and before returning to work; parents may go back to work part-time in order to be with the baby more; the costs of raising a child are significant: clothes, childcare, equipment etc. all signifies a leap in costs. It may also be that parents have to move to larger accommodation in order to house the growing family.

Research activity

Spend some time researching benefits and financial matters, ensuring that you have up-to-date materials that parents can take away with them. They are likely to be:

- government based information on benefits and parental and maternity rights and payments;
- local authority publications giving advice on local information and support;
- local organisations that support parents, either through an advisory service such as Citizens Advice Bureau, or local networking groups who offer social support.

Review all your materials to ensure that you have the correct information available.

Returning to work can bring with it many worries, even though it can also relieve financial pressures. A survey carried out by the National Childbirth Trust in 2008 asked mothers about their experiences of returning to work. Its Executive Summary noted that:

despite the strengthened legislation and often enhanced benefits, this survey has found that one in three women (39%) find it difficult or very difficult to return to work after maternity leave. The cost of a difficult transition back to work is not only personal it also affects the team and organisation for which they work.

(NCT, 2008, p. 3)

Although the survey was not representative of all mothers returning to work as two thirds of the women held professional or managerial posts, it is likely that these are the women who would be using childcare in terms of affordability and salary profile. The survey also recognises the bias in its sample towards married women.

The most common concern about returning to work was childcare (60%), followed by:

- time to do everything (57%);
- missing my child (56%);
- my child missing me (53%);
- ability to be a good mother (47%) (National Childbirth Trust, 2008, p. 9).

⚡ Short activity: Supporting the return to work

Having looked at the issues that concern parents, reflect upon some of the ways that you might be able to address these issues (e.g. 'my child missing me'; 'being a good mother'). How can you reassure parents that they are indeed good mothers and that their child does not miss them too much during the day?

Discuss and consider how you can approach this.

Traumatic birth and returning to work

As well as the challenges of returning to work, the physical impact of giving birth may be something that practitioners are not aware of.

🔍 CASE STUDY

Sarah has a four month old baby, Jemima, who is healthy and lively. Sarah is returning to work and has decided to use a childminder (Suraya) as her main form of childcare, with her mother-in-law (Tina) providing an extra day's care when needed. Sarah is going back to work for three days a week

continued

so will use the childminder then, and her mother-in-law will look after Jemima when she increases her work to four days a week in two months' time.

Unknown to Surayah, Sarah experienced a traumatic birth, requiring surgery immediately after the birth to secure a tear, and then further surgery two months ago when an infection set in.

Sarah is in discomfort most of the time and has problems with bladder incontinence now. She has not seen anyone to talk about the birth to, although this was offered by the hospital. Her view is that 'least said, soonest mended', although her partner does encourage Sarah to get some help as it is affecting their relationship. Tina has mentioned that Sarah is having trouble 'down there' to Suraya, unbeknown to Sarah. While Sarah tries not to let the constant pain and anxiety about leaks affect her, she does occasionally snap at both the baby and the childminder.

As a practitioner, what action, if any, would you take in this situation? How might you adapt your practice in the future?

Reflection on case study

This case study may have stimulated discussions about boundaries: how far to intervene; what are the acceptable practices in supporting parents; when do minor concerns about potential safeguarding become opportunities to activate intervention strategies; what are the facts about traumatic births and the impact they might have upon new mothers?

The Birth Trauma Association asserts that:

> It is estimated that, in the UK alone, this may result in up to 20,000 women a year developing Post Traumatic Stress Disorder (PTSD).

> Also, as many as 200,000 more women may feel traumatised by childbirth and develop some of the symptoms of PTSD.

> (Birth Trauma Association, 2017)

Statistically, it is likely that mothers who have experienced a traumatic birth will visit a childcare setting before they return to work. It is neither possible not desirable to know the obstetric history of all mothers who visit nurseries but it is in the interests of nurseries to make the setting a place where the traumas and medical (physical and emotional) challenges of childbirth and the neonatal period are recognised and understood, even without this being overtly stated. This can be achieved in a number of ways, including making materials such as leaflets available for new parents to access.

Supporting breastfeeding in the nursery

Your setting can find out more about parental rights and breastfeeding from organisations including the Health and Safety Executive (www.hse.gov.uk).

Mothers are entitled to breastfeed in their place of work and express milk to leave in a nursery for you to give to the baby. Many babies who start at nursery will find it difficult to tolerate a bottle, especially with so many other changes going on in their lives.

Longer activity: Breastfeeding in the nursery

This is a letter to a new mum's website and highlights some of the problems that parents can have when returning to work. After you have read it, think about the practices you have in place in your setting.

My daughter has not long started at nursery (3 weeks ago) and is doing 3 full days a week. Her settling in sessions didn't go too badly and I explained how I'd been expressing every day and night to build up a supply in the freezer so I could carry on when back at work. I also explained that Cherry (name changed) had never accepted a bottle, we had tried and tried all different types of scenario and bottles, but she just isn't interested so I said I'd prefer milk to be given in a sippy cup as I've had some success with her having milk from it.

Anyway when I went to pick her up last week they said they'd tried to give her a bottle . . . they said they persevered with it but she got 'very tearful' so they didn't try again, which meant she went from half 8 till half 3 with nothing (she isn't quite 6 months old yet) and I have only just started giving the occasional solids over the past week but . . . they said they'd tried to spoon feed her some mash and gravy which she had a few bites of.

continued

This morning I dropped her off and had a word with the manager of the place and said I didn't want her to be forced with a bottle and had provided a cup for her (as I had done from the start anyway) and the manager asked if she'd ever had a bottle, I said no (maybe that's my own fault for not introducing one when she was really little) and then she said have you tried xxx (formula brand), she will probably take it – I was like, erm . . . what has that got to do with anything? She said, well you're bound to be stopping now and giving follow on milk as she's approaching 6 months and I said no I was going to carry on until she didn't want the boob anymore. She just nodded at me so I went in to drop her off and gave the girl looking after the room today more frozen breast milk as there was still milk left over from yesterday and she asked where her bottle was . . . Cue more repeating what I'd said about a cup and she asked me why I won't give her a bottle. Cue more explaining and she said oh right, we don't have any other breastfeeders . . . All during this baby is crying and I'm struggling with leaving her anyway, but it's making me feel paranoid and like I'm some kind of weirdo for not giving formula . . . I don't have anything against formula feeding at all but breastfeeding has just worked so well for us, but I feel like they think I'm some kind of snob and being difficult as I don't want her having formula (she has a suspected cow's milk intolerance and eczema) or a bottle . . .

I'm sure I'm thinking this is all a lot worse than maybe it is as it's been a bad few days with baby spending the whole day pretty much in tears (after her settling had gone so well) and probably me being hormonal but would you say something or wait a bit longer?

(Edited version of community post reproduced with permission of BabyCenter, L.L.C.)

In groups, discuss what this setting could be doing differently.

Create your own breastfeeding policy

Do you have a breastfeeding policy? This might be an effective way to clarify expectations with staff and to demonstrate to breastfeeding parents that they are welcomed and that there is a good understanding of the particular issues relating to breastfed babies managing the transition to nursery. Under the Equality Act 2010, it is illegal to discriminate against mothers who are breastfeeding a child. Given, therefore, that mothers are entitled to feed their babies in your setting, is there a space to provide a comfortable feeding chair?

There are a number of breastfeeding policies online, and most of them will cover:

- breastfeeding on the premises;
- how and where expressed breastmilk (EBM) can be stored;
- guidance on handling EBM;
- sharing feeding routines;
- labelling of EBM;
- defrosting, storage and disposal of EBM.

Postnatal depression

'The effect of persistent postnatal depression on children is a major public health issue' (Stein *et al.*, 2018 p. 134). This recent study undertook research into postnatal depression (PND) and found that 'postnatal depression can have wide-ranging negative effects on child development. In early childhood, these effects include impairments in cognitive performance, behaviour disturbance, and insecurity of attachment' (Stein *et al.*, 2018, p. 134). It can be very difficult to spot the symptoms of postnatal depression during the short meetings that you might have with parents, especially if they do not want to share this information with you.

However, it affects more than one in ten women within a year of giving birth (NHS, 2016), therefore it is likely that in most nurseries you will be working with parents who are suffering from PND.

Chapter review

See Table 6.6, p. 102.

RESOURCES **TABLE 6.6** Practice review

Chapter section	Fully engaged with strategies in place	Somewhat engaged	Further development needed
Trust building			
Attachment and separation			
Sleep and fatigue			
Work and finance			
Traumatic birth			
Supporting breastfeeding			
Postnatal depression			
Reflection on chapter			
What changes have you made?			
What needs further development?			

Further reading

Birth Trauma Association

www.birthtraumaassociation.org.uk/

Three main areas:

(1) Raising awareness of birth trauma
(2) Working to prevent it
(3) Supporting families in need

Breastfeeding

World Health Organisation Breastfeeding Guidelines

www.who.int/mediacentre/news/statements/2011/breastfeeding_20110115/en/

National Childbirth Trust

Leaflet on expressing and storing breastmilk: www.nct.org.uk/sites/default/files/related_documents/Expressing%20and%20storing%20your%20breastmilk.pdf

NHS leaflet on expressing and storing breastmilk: www.nhs.uk/Conditions/pregnancy-and-baby/Pages/expressing-storing-breast-milk.aspx

The Breastfeeding Network

www.breastfeedingnetwork.org.uk

Health and Safety Executive

FAQs for parents who will breastfeed on returning to work: www.hse.gov.uk/mothers/faqs.htm#q14

ACAS

Information about breastfeeding in the workplace from ACAS: http://m.acas.org.uk/media/pdf/b/s/Acas-guide-on-accommodating-breastfeeding-in-the-workplace.pdf

Postnatal support

National Childbirth Trust: www.nct.org.uk

Parenting classes

Parenting classes can be found online, but there are a huge variety and many of them are expensive. Some classes can be sourced through the local authority. It is advisable to find classes that have some evidence-based information that will support their effectiveness.

CAN Parent courses: www.parentinguk.org/canparent

The database www.parentinguk.org/canparent/parenting-courses/ helps you find some of the parenting classes currently available in the UK. Classes with the CANparent logo have acquired the CANparent quality mark for universal parenting classes.

References

Birth Trauma Association (2017). Home Page Online: www.birthtraumaassociation.org.uk/

Bowlby, J. (1997) Attachment *and loss, V1: Attachment.* London: Hogarth Press.

Department for Education (DfE) (2017). *Statutory framework for the early years foundation stage.* London: DfE.

Howe, D. (2011). *Attachment across the life course.* London: Palgrave Macmillan.

National Childbirth Trust (2008). *The experiences of women returning to work after maternity leave in the UK: A summary of survey results.* London: NCT. Online: www.nct.org.uk/sites/default/files/related_documents/ReturningToWork-Survey.pdf

National College for Teaching and Leadership (NCTL) (2013). *Teachers' standards (early years).* Retrieved from: https://www.gov.uk/government/uploads/system/uploads/attachment_data/file/211646/Early_Years_Teachers__Standards.pdf

National Health Service (2016). *Postnatal depression.* Online: www.nhs.uk/conditions/post-natal-depression/

Office for Standards in Education (Ofsted) (2018). *Early years inspection handbook.* London: Ofsted.

Sadeh, A., Tikotzky, L. & Scher, A., (2010). Parenting and infant sleep. *Sleep Medicine Reviews, 14,* 89–96.

Stein, A., Netsi, E., Lawrence, P.J., Granger, C., Kempton, C., Craske, M. G., Nickless, A., Mollison, J., Stewart, D.A., Rapa, E., West, V., Scerif, G., Cooper, P.J. & Murray, L. (2018). Mitigating the effect of persistent postnatal depression on child outcomes through an intervention to treat depression and improve parenting: a randomised controlled trial. *The Lancet Psychiatry, 5* (2), 134–144.

van der Helm, E., Gujar, N. & Walker, M.P. (2010). Sleep deprivation impairs the accurate recognition of human emotions. *Sleep, 3* (3), 335–342.

7 | Parental engagement in the toddler room

TABLE 7.1 Links to EY documentation

Teachers' Standards (Early Years), (NCTL, 2013)	Early years inspection handbook (Ofsted, updated 2018)	*Statutory framework for early years foundation stage (DfE, 2017)*
1.2 2.1 3.1 6.1	s. 154, p. 35 s. 155, pp. 36–37	s. 2.3 and 2.4 p. 13 s. 2.5 p. 14

As children become more mobile, so they may transition from a baby room, where infants and young children are less mobile, spending much of their time sitting up, crawling or lying down, to a room that can accommodate more active behaviour. This may mean that the child and parents will be leaving a key person behind and getting to know a new group of practitioners with slightly different routines. You will find more information on transitions in Chapter 5. This chapter looks at the unique opportunities and characteristics that may play a part in the relationships that practitioners have with parents of toddlers (Table 7.2).

In this chapter, the focus will include:

- play and development;
- opportunities to share between setting and home;
- learning social skills, managing behaviour;
- arrival of new siblings;
- emergent language, literacy and numeracy;
- parenting styles.

TABLE 7.2 Practice reflection

Chapter section	Fully engaged with strategies in place	Somewhat engaged	Further development needed
Play and developing ideas together			
Sharing information			
Learning social skills; managing behaviour			
Emergent literacy and numeracy			
What strategies are currently in place?			
What needs further development?			

Overnight reflection

Think about a time when you have worked closely with parents to develop a particular aspect of the child's social development – this could be something that you or the parents feel needs some attention (such as dealing with tantrums). How did you broach the topic to the parents in the first instance? What was your relationship with the parents like before you had this discussion? Are there any parents that you would hesitate to raise issues with? What tips would you share?

Being the parent of a toddler

The age of the children in the toddler room will vary from setting to setting, depending on staffing, space and ratio requirements, setting preferences and numbers of children. It is likely to be from the age when a child starts to walk competently and therefore is able to function in a more social and mobile world, until they reach the pre-school year where new skills will be acquired to manage the demands of school readiness. The play opportunities that were available while sitting or crawling explode, while all the time they grapple with mastery of their physical and interactive challenges.

This room is a busy, noisy, emotional room with, from time to time, the associated anarchy of the uninitiated youngster who is not much more than an infant and has yet to work out 'the rules of the game'. At this point, children start a more active socialisation process. Having moved out of the baby phase of observing behaviour with little control or autonomy over their own engagement, they are now active participants, able to join in and play socially, all the while learning the expectations of social behaviour in the only way possible – through experience.

For the parent, being responsible for a toddler brings with it a new set of challenges, as the developmental phases start to really take off. Again, a useful topic to think about is: how will this feel for the parent? There are opportunities to capture this information during the progress check, which takes place between two and three years.

The practitioner in the toddler room has a delicate path to tread: managing the highs and lows of toddler development, sharing information with parents and using the information they receive from parents but also, importantly, reassuring and informing parents that their child's development is, generally, nothing to worry about.

Play

While play is a fundamental element of children's development from infancy, it could be argued that the toddler years are where play comes into its own and can be used in countless ways to progress children's imagination, language, sociability, numeracy and physical development (Andrews, 2012). As children become more independent physically and start to develop more sophisticated cognitive and social skills, the skilled support of play activities can help development to blossom. This focus on play can be shared in so many ways with parents, to the benefit of children, with playful opportunities that can flow between home and setting, supporting many different areas of development. The *Development Matters* document (Early Education, 2012) is something that you probably use to help guide your own assessment of children development and to work with parents. There are many suggestions of the ways that adults can cooperate and adapt environments in the **Positive Relationships** and **Enabling Environment** sections to support play and development.

One classical theorist working in this field was Mildred Parten (1932), who recognized six different types of play:

- unoccupied (play) – often seen with babies;
- solitary (independent) play – no attempts to interact;

- onlooker play (behaviour) – watching others;
- parallel play – independent play but alongside others;
- associative play – sharing materials, discussing but not organised together;
- cooperative play – using groups, division of labour, a shared goal.

More recently, Bob Hughes' taxonomy of play types, as cited in Andrews (2012, p. 32), shows a wider range of play types (see Table 7.3).

Longer activity: Play types

In the main group (or in smaller groups if preferred), look at the list in Table 7.3, and check that you understand all the types of play so you can share with parents. Think of an example that you could pass on to parents for them to look out for at home. Ask parents to take photos of these activities from home and add them to learning journeys.

TABLE 7.3 Types of play: activity

Type of play	Give an example that could be transferred to home
Symbolic	
Rough and tumble	
Socio-dramatic	
Social	
Creative	
Communication	
Dramatic	
Deep	
Exploratory	
Fantasy	
Imaginative	
Locomotor	
Mastery	
Object	
Role-play	
Recapitulative	

Developing ideas

You probably use a similar form in your setting, but Table 7.4 is an example of something that can be used to share ideas with parents. You can print off a few and leave them for parents to collect, or create documents and send them online. Make sure that you use reputable and research based information for your play ideas, such as the National Health Services, 4Children, Early Education. By doing this, you are demonstrating partnership values and encouraging parental engagement. It will help you become more familiar with parents and will help you to identify family interests.

Play is just one area where the engagement of parents can aid in the development of the learning. In the Pen Green Children's Centre in Nottinghamshire, sharing ideas with parents has been a long-term focus and has resulted in strong partnership work. (Whalley, Arnold & Orr, 2013). In their book, they talk about the different ways that they make connections with parents on issues of development:

Pen Green engaged 89 per cent of nursery and Baby Nest parents in the following ways:

- by sharing sessions on key child development concepts – developing a shared language for thinking about children's learning;
- daily dialogues achieved via flexible starts and finishes to the day;
- diaries;
- weekly study groups: am and pm and evening;
- portfolios of children's learning;
- sharing DVD vignettes of children's learning in the home and in the nursery;
- annual trips to the science museum with parents, staff and children;
- open evenings focusing on key learning issues;
- Pen Green staff publishing their work alongside parents.

(Whalley *et al.*, 2013, p. 5)

Longer activity: Ideas about play

How do you share information about play or other aspects of development with parents? Are there any aspects of the Pen Green work that you are doing? What else are you doing that involves sharing learning with parents? What do you think would be possible, and how would you be able to make it work for you? Give yourself plenty of time for this activity – some things may seem impossible but it may just require a little planning. Use this to do some blue-sky thinking, with groups, collecting information on flip chart paper or on the ideas page. Why not also send some of the Pen Green ideas out to parents, asking them what they would like to see?

TABLE 7.4 Play ideas for toddlers: activity

Activity	Preparation	What to do
Using playdough	1 cup plain flour 1 tbsp. oil 1 cup water 1/2 cup salt 2 tbsp. cream of tartar Food colouring (opt)	Make shapes Feel it, squish it Let children feel the sensations as they squeeze it through their fingers.
What do we think about this:	*Katy in Blossoms Room says:* This activity is so popular with our children. They love to make shapes with it and put it into feeders and see what shape comes out. It is good for children because it helps to develop their **Fine Motor Skills (Physical Development).** It is good for children because it helps to **learn new language: squish, splat, gooey, gloopy (communication and language)** **Two more with links to areas of development** The salt in the recipe should stop them from eating it but never leave your child alone when doing this.	
Did you and your child enjoy doing this activity?	*Yes, Juliana loved squashing the shapes after I made them in the playdoh machine. She also liked to hold it up in the air and let it fall to the table.*	
What did your child do?	*As the playdoh dropped, she said 'drop, drop' as she watch it. Then she said 'oh dear' as she squashed the shapes.*	
Any other ideas	*Are there any songs we could sing while we do this? Maybe you have some ideas of songs you sing at nursery that we can copy at home?*	
Date shared	**Next steps:**	

CASE STUDY

Nasreen works in the toddler room and one of her key families, who has just come from the baby room, is from Somalia. Mum speaks little English and never stops to talk. Nasreen has been thinking about different ways to draw her in, and, as Asad still has an afternoon sleep, Nasreen does some research on songs and lullabies in Somali, then she asks mum and dad to drop by some time. At first they don't take any notice of her but then she sends another message and explains why she wanted to talk to them. They are delighted to hear the Somali songs and mention that they live with older family who would also know these songs and who don't have to work. Nasreen persuades them to ask Asad's grandparents to come in and sing the songs. It turns out that Asad's grandmother was in the local choir when living in Somalia so she has a strong voice and is confident to come along and sing some songs. Asad loves seeing his grandmother with the other children at nursery and you can see him bursting with pride and singing along when his 'ayeeyo' comes to visit. Nasreen takes photos of the day and puts them on the noticeboard.

This gets Nasreen thinking. She sends out a message to all parents about the songs they sing to their children and asks them to talk to her. As a result, she gathers a range of songs from many different countries: Ireland, Poland, France, Somalia, England and Scotland. Then she makes a recording of it and plays it to the children regularly. Children hear the songs they hear at home and they share them in the setting, giving them a wider understanding of the world and different languages.

Sharing information

Two-year-old progress check

This is not the only time when the sharing of information is an essential part of working with parents; however, this chapter will focus on the ways to build, maintain and improve relationships during this phase, mainly because there is an important shared assessment (the two-year-old progress check).

The purpose of the two-year-old progress check is to share information when the child is between 24 and 36 months and gather a clear developmental picture in the three prime areas of the EYFS:

- Social and emotional development
- Physical development
- Communication and language.

The aims of the progress check are to:

- review a child's development in the three prime areas of the EYFS;
- ensure that parents have a clear picture of their child's development;
- enable practitioners to understand the child's needs and plan activities to meet them in the setting;
- enable parents to understand the child's needs and, with support from practitioners, enhance development at home;
- note areas where a child is progressing well and identify any areas where progress is less than expected; and
- describe actions the provider intends to take to address any developmental concerns (including working with other professionals where appropriate).

(NCB, 2012, p. 3)

The NCB guide, available through the Foundation Years website (see link in references), gives you all the information you need about the progress and purpose of the check, and helps practitioners to see the importance of working closely with parents and children. It also goes into detail about building partnerships.

There is a section entitled: 'What do parents want from the progress check', which states that:

The most useful and valuable summaries will:

- be clear and easy to read;
- be easy to understand, avoiding unfamiliar jargon, acronyms or terminology (with interpretation and translation available where appropriate);
- present a truthful yet sensitive reflection of what the child can do and their achievements to date; identify areas where the child is progressing at a slower pace than expected;
- recognise parents' in-depth knowledge of their child by incorporating their observations and comments;
- give parents an idea of how their child's development will be taken forward in the setting;
- provide some suggestions for parents in supporting their child at home; and
- reflect their child's individual personality and characteristics.

(NCB, 2012, pp. 10–11)

Learning social skills; managing behaviour

This is possibly the most challenging aspect of working with parents because of the wide range of expectations of children's behaviour, especially if you are working in a setting that is culturally diverse. It is the area where your skills of managing judgements on parents will be much needed, and you may find some surprises and adjustments to any stereotyping that you may have about behaviour. Your goal might be to understand the position of parents in respect of their backgrounds rather than attributing any responsibility to perceived lapses in behaviour management. In terms of cultural constructs, there is no right or wrong here. However, you will be maintaining vigilance in terms of safeguarding and will be aware of expectations that might need to be reported.

The identification of parenting style as an indicator of children's outcomes has been understood for some decades and continues to be used as an effective indicator (Majumder, 2016). Styles of parenting, according to this model, can vary according to two factors:

- degree of warmth;
- degree of control.

In Figure 7.1, you can see that parenting with a high level of warmth but a low level of control would sit within the box labelled 'permissive'. Conversely, a style with high control and low warmth would be authoritarian. You may recognise these styles and

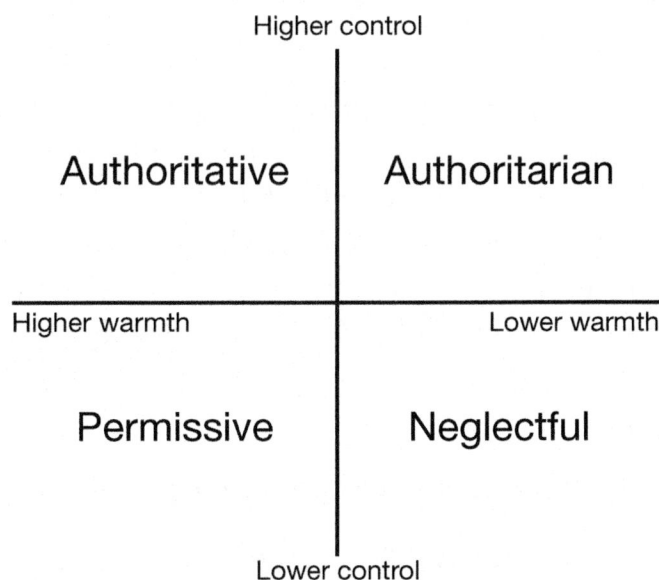

FIGURE 7.1 Parenting styles

Based on Maccoby and Martin (1983) and Baumrind's (1991) four parenting styles

be able to imagine parents in your setting who display these characteristics. You may also see that the most effective parenting style is one that has a higher level of control (therefore with boundaries in place) but also a high level of warmth, so boundaries but within a loving relationship.

CASE STUDY

Ewan's behaviour has changed recently – he has lost his appetite and will not play with his friends, preferring to sit alone with a collection of his favourite toy cars. Sometimes, he drives the car along the floor very fast making racing noises as he goes, and bashing the heels of anyone who is in his path. Luckily their shoes prevent any serious damage but Ewan's key person knows that he needs to get to the bottom of the causes of this behaviour.

The key person wonders whether Ewan is unsettled as his parents have been going through a separation recently. The key person knows that they are quite 'laissez-faire' when it comes to boundaries with Ewan but they are also clearly both under stress.

- **What do you advise the KP to do?**

- **What do you think he may discover?**

- **What can happen next?**

In order to build relationships with parents, sensitivity and understanding is required. It is quite probable that you are seeing parents at their stressed-out worst on bad days, as they hand over or pick up at the end of busy working days. The previous activity perhaps highlighted the importance of helping parents to see things in a different light, and being patient and understanding. This activity will do the same, if you have some extroverts who will play the parts while others give them guidance on what to say!

Longer activity: Role-play – being non-judgemental

This is an activity where the more confident practitioners can act out the role-play, trying out a range of different approaches. The rest of the group can watch and make suggestions about the direction of the conversation. You might want to do a 'how not to do this' before you work on a 'doing it the respectful way'.

Parent: This is Tom, breadwinner, single parent of two children who also lives with his own mother, who is elderly and currently suffering from heart disease. She would normally help with childcare but has not been able to for the past two weeks. Dad is running late because it is the end of the tax year and he works in an accountant's office – when it is like this, there is no possibility of leaving on time, and he hasn't had a chance to ring the nursery. Oh well, he is that frazzled that he has not even the energy to be worried about it. All he knows is that it is likely to happen again tomorrow.

Practitioner: This is Jan, at the end of the day, and most of the children have gone home, but Sammi is still here. The same thing happened yesterday but it wasn't so late. Sammi is tired and earlier on, he tried to bite one of the children. Luckily someone noticed this before any damage was done. Jan is thinking about how she can avoid sounding cross but knows that she has to tell dad straight away – or does she?

- **Discuss different options and how they might act out.**

- **Role-play them and see what seems to work best.**

Emergent language, literacy and numeracy

Another area of development within the toddler years is the early stage of reading, writing and mathematics. Parents often find that the developmental stages leading to language, literacy and numeracy seem to be completely disconnected to the final outcome, and they can feel that the sooner their child puts a pen in their hand, the more satisfied they will be with the work that takes place in the nursery. It is therefore for the nursery to share the important information relating to development so that parents are introduced to this at an early stage. In other words, children playing in the sand, putting their hands into water, paint and mud and making shapes with their fingers, putting boxes on top of each other and so on, are all part of developing these skills. For parents, it may not seem obvious, but the more they are engaged with the setting in relation to learning and development, the more aware they will become, and their involvement is a key element in the acquisition of learning. The longitudinal study 'Effective provision of pre-school practice' (Sylva *et al.*, 2004) shows that family background doesn't make any difference – it is what the family does – so practitioners who support parents in developing the home learning environment can open up further opportunities for learning.

Beware of promoting the 'deficit' model to families

However, 'there can be a thin line between acknowledging that poverty can undermine achievement and adopting interventions designed to compensate for parents' supposed shortcomings that promote a deficit model of families' (Feiler, 2005, p. 133). In other words, good practice means avoiding being an 'expert' and making pronouncements to parents. You can relate this to the previous activities in this section, looking at how to listen and discuss changes in behaviour that might affect children, and maintaining a non-judgement approach, using a strength-based practice approach (see Chapter 3). For example, the desired outcome is to encourage parents to engage with the setting rather them make them feel guilty or inadequate. This can help in unexpected ways; for example, in one study, a mother was in a nursery observing a researcher reading with a child. She noticed that the researcher was using probing questions. After she saw that, the mother added probing questions herself when reading to her child. 'In this case, access to professional knowledge through incidental observation had a significant impact, one that was unintended by the researcher' (McNaughton, 2001, pp. 48–49).

Here is another example:

> In the descriptive study by Goodridge and McNaughton (1994), families in relatively poorer communities of Auckland were asked to provide examples of the writing of their four and a half year old children. Initially, they could provide very few instances. When the request was pursued, by asking for drawings, scribbling, joint activities and other emergent writing attempts, we received many examples. Initially, the parents did not hold the same views of the significance of these activities as the researchers did, but could quickly find examples of writing activities with a shared views.
>
> (McNaughton, 2001, p. 49)

This study illustrates the way that practitioners can introduce ideas about development with families in order that they can share outcomes and recognise progress.

Further reading

There are many different and helpful sources of information on how to share play ideas with parents on the internet, for example:

Gill, T. (2007). No fear: Growing up in a risk averse society. www.dad.info/kids/children/5-simple-steps-to-help-get-the-kids-back-in-their-usual-sleep-routine

NHS: Children under five years: www.nhs.uk/Livewell/fitness/Documents/children-under-5-years.pdf

RESOURCES

TABLE 7.5 Practice review

Chapter section	Fully engaged with strategies in place	Somewhat engaged	Further development needed
Play and developing ideas together			
Sharing information			
Learning social skills; managing behaviour			
Emergent literacy and numeracy			
Reflection on chapter			
What changes have you made?			
What needs further development?			

NHS: Play ideas and reading: www.nhs.uk/conditions/pregnancy-and-baby/play-ideas-and-reading/?#close

Materials to support the process of ongoing assessment in the EYFS are available at: www.foundationyears.org.uk/

Resources to support practice in listening to young children include the 'Listening to young children' series of leaflets. These are available at: www.ncb.org.uk/ycvn/resources/listening-as-a-way-of-life

References

4Children (2015). *What to expect, when: Guidance to your child's learning and development in the early years foundation stage.* London: 4children.

Andrews, M. (2012). *Exploring play for early childhood studies.* London: SAGE.

Baumrind, D. (1991). The influence of parenting style on adolescence competence and substance use. *Journal of Early Adolescence, 11,* 56–95.

Department for Education (DfE) (2017). *Statutory framework for the early years foundation stage.* London: DfE.

Early Education. (2012). *Development matters in the early years foundation stage.* London: Early Education.

Feiler, A. (2005). Linking home and school literacy in an inner city reception class. *Journal of Early Childhood Literacy, 5* (2), 131–149.

Foundation Years (2013). *Good practice support in sharing information.* Available at: www.foundationyears.org.uk/files/2013/11/Good_Practice_Support_in_Information_Sharing.pdf

Maccoby, E.E. & Martin, J.A. (1983). Socialization in the context of the family: Parent–child interaction. In E.M. Hetherington (ed.) *Handbook of child psychology: Socialization, personality and social development.* Vol. 4. New York: Wiley.

McNaughton, S. (2001). Co-constructing expertise: The development of parents' and teachers' ideas about literacy practices and transition to school. *Journal of Early Childhood Literacy, 1* (1), 40–58.

Majumder, M.A. (2016). The impact of parenting style on children's educational outcomes in the United States. *Journal of Family Economic Issues, 37,* 89–98.

National Children's Bureau (2012). *Know how: The progress check at age two.* London: NCB/DfE. Available at: www.foundationyears.org.uk/files/2012/03/A-Know-How-Guide.pdf

National College for Teaching and Leadership (NCTL) (2013). *Teachers' standards (early years).* Retrieved from: https://www.gov.uk/government/uploads/system/uploads/attachment_data/file/211646/Early_Years_Teachers__Standards.pdf

Office for Standards in Education (Ofsted) (2018). *Early years inspection handbook. London:* Ofsted.

Parten, M.B. (1932). Social participation among pre-school children. *Journal of Abnormal and Social Psychology, 27,* 243–269.

Sylva, K., Melhuish, E., Sammons, P., Siraj-Blatchford, I. & Taggart, B. (2004). *The effective provision of pre-school education (EPPE): Project Final Report. A longitudinal evaluation (1997–2004).* London: DfES.

Whalley, M., Arnold, C., & Orr, R. (eds) (2013). *Working with families in children's centres and early years settings.* London: Hodder Education.

8 | Parental engagement in the pre-school room

TABLE 8.1 Links to EY documentation

Teachers' Standards (Early Years), (NCTL, 2013)	Early years inspection handbook (Ofsted, updated 2018)	*Statutory framework for early years foundation stage (DfE, 2017)*
2.4 3.3 4.5 5.1 6.2	s. 147 (p. 29) s. 153 (p. 33) s. 155 (p. 36) s. 157 (p. 38)	s. 2.1 (p. 13) s. 2.6 (p. 14) s. 2.9 (p. 14)

This chapter provides a number of activities and points for reflection that can help practitioners understand the range of needs of parents whose children are approaching school age (Table 8.2). It will make use of current research to support training in the needs of parents of pre-schoolers, the focus including:

- What's happening in the pre-school phase
- Developing dialogues to engage parents with the move to school
- Sharing observations and assessments for transition
- School readiness
- Saying goodbye

Overnight reflection

What does school readiness mean to you as a practitioner?

This will be discussed in an activity towards the end of this chapter – see p. 130.

RESOURCES TABLE 8.2 Practice reflection

Chapter section	Fully engaged with strategies in place	Somewhat engaged	Further development needed
What's happening in the pre-school phase			
Developing dialogues with parents			
Sharing observation and assessments			
School readiness			
Saying goodbye			
What strategies are currently in place?			
What needs further development?			

What's happening in the pre-school phase?

As children's development continues, so the opportunities to increase physical skills, expand vocabulary and increase social understanding continue to present themselves. At this stage, children are developing their sense of ownership of their environment and the characteristics of effective learning (DfE, 2017), will be evident in many aspects of their play-based activities. Children in this phase may also be being encouraged to start preparing for their move to school, probably to a reception class. However, the philosophy of play-based learning will remain as the dominant driver of activities, while building on children's learning dispositions as stated in the *Statutory Framework for the Early Years Foundation Stage*.

Three characteristics of effective teaching and learning are:

- **Playing and exploring** – children investigate and experience things, and 'have a go'.
- **Active learning** – children concentrate and keep on trying if they encounter difficulties, and enjoy achievements.
- **Creating and thinking critically** – children have and develop their own ideas, make links between ideas, and develop strategies for doing things.

(DfE, 2017, p. 10)

These are all areas where parental involvement can add a cultural richness to a setting, where children's experiences beyond the setting can be articulated by them (and their families) to the nursery community in order to learn about the range of traditions, learning methods, play opportunities that can be shared and celebrated. This in turn will help children to value their own experiences and uniqueness and it offers another opportunity to reach out to all parents and invite them to become part of the setting. Again, remember that the parents who do not engage may have many reasons for their absence: they could feel that they won't have enough of value to offer; they may feel embarrassed and anxious that their literacy or numeracy skills are lacking; they may come from a cultural background where it is not expected that parents engage with education; they may be too busy in their working responsibilities but engage in their children's learning at home; they may also feel that they do not fit into the setting and have different understandings of the level of involvement welcomed (Erdreich & Golden, 2016; Lareau, 1987).

Longer activity: Sharing learning with parents

This activity is aimed at generating ideas to share what you are doing with parents at this stage. Using the characteristics of teaching and early learning and the areas of learning and development, share ideas with parents to complete the grid in Table 8.3. Work in small groups and use the 'Development Matters' document (Early Education, 2012) as a guide. This is also a way of sharing observations and assessments, which will feed into the development of new activities and challenges. You should agree with them the best way of sharing with parents; you could complete it together or you could send it to the parents with the first example completed and then ask them to complete the rest from their perspective.

The form shown in Table 8.3 can be used by parents and practitioners to share ideas of children's interests and recent activities. You could complete it across a week or a month and then compare notes. It might be useful to add some guidance to the headings so parents are clear about what is meant.

TABLE 8.3 Sharing learning with parents: activity

Child's name	Playing and exploring	Active Learning	Creating and thinking critically
Week/Month:			
Physical development			
Personal, social & emotional development			
Communication & language			
Literacy			
Mathematics			
Understanding the world			
Expressive arts & design			
Comments from parents			
Comments from practitioners			

Developing dialogues to engage parents with assessment and the move to school

Just as other ages can bring with them challenges (returning to work after a baby; managing two children; behavioural challenges), so the pre-school phase is no different. Additionally, any of these challenges can take place at any time so there is no set formula to prepare for challenges.

However, one pressure that might be present during the pre-school phase is the feeling that children should be preparing for school and of course, that must mean the end of play-based learning. Sharing activities such as the one above can help parents to realise that play-based learning is an essential part of all of the EYFS, not just the earlier stages. Again, good communication with families will improve trust and support parents' confidence in the evidence base that has been used to develop the EYFS.

If you are holding a parent's evening during this time, you might want to gauge how parents are feeling about their children starting school. One way to do this would be to send out a sheet to complete (see next activity, Table 8.4) prior to any meeting. Although you may have your own ideas on the concerns of parents, this way you will have written evidence that this has come from parents and it is also a way for you to be sure and to be able to support the parents in managing these concerns.

My child is starting school!

Dear parents,

Before our next meeting, it would be helpful if you could complete this form after talking to your child about how they are feeling about starting school.

Thank you

TABLE 8.4 My child is starting school: activity

Name of child	
Date	
We hope that starting school will be:	We are concerned that starting school might be:

Acknowledging parents' hopes and fears

When you talk to parents about their aspirations and concerns, it helps to acknowledge their feelings, reflecting back what they express. Here are some useful phrases that you can use when talking to parents:

- So you have some thoughts about the transition to school?

- Can you tell me about them, for example, this one? (from sheet)

- Yes, I see what you mean

- So, you say that . . . (reflecting/repeating back what parent has said to you)? (no need to say any more – they will pick up the thread)

- So, am I right in thinking that you feel . . .? (summarising what you have heard)

- Do you have any thoughts on how you'd like to manage this?

- What sounds right for you?

- These are some possible suggestions

- In my experience, some parents find that xxxxx can help.

- Someone I know felt exactly like this – I know that they tried xxxx – do you think that might help you?

🕐 Longer activity: Role-play on hopes and fears

Before this session starts, ask half of the training group to complete the 'Hopes and fears about starting school' sheet (Table 8.4) as though they were a parent, and the other half to look at the phrases above and keep them in mind for this activity. When you run this activity in the session set up the group in pairs, with each pair having a 'parent' (who has already completed the form) and a 'practitioner'.

In pairs (with a 'parent' and a 'practitioner' in each pair), spend 5–8 minutes talking about the parents' hopes and fears about starting school. The goal is to reassure parents, but also to let them know that you value their comments and will give them further information about their concerns if needed.

After you have completed the activity, discuss in the main group how this went, and whether there are any ideas for pre-empting the fears.

The purpose of this activity is to help parents manage their anxieties before they change settings, and to show them that you understand how they might be feeling. For the practitioners in the role-play, one thing that they should avoid doing is to say 'Oh you don't need to worry about that'. This will lead to a breakdown in trust as parents may feel that you are dismissing their fears. There are other ways to manage fears that you can agree with parents.

At the end of the activity, it would be helpful to give feedback to the practitioner about how reassured and supported the parent felt.

FAQ sheets

By the end of these activities with parents, you will have plenty of information about the hopes and fears of parents. Share this information (anonymously of course) by creating an FAQ sheet of both the hopes and the fears and the solutions that you agreed with the parents. Many of these feelings will be commonly shared so this will offer reassurance to parents.

Case studies for discussion

These case studies can be used with practitioners who are working in a reception class once children have transferred into school:

CASE STUDY 1

Marta Kaminski works as in a reception class of a primary school in a multicultural town and, as someone who moved to the UK from Poland, has a strong empathy with families using English as an additional language.
She has lived here since 2005 and has successfully been granted British citizenship.

As a way of getting to know her pupils better, Marta organises home visits for new families and she strives to speak to parents regularly about their children's progress. Whilst she is a popular and effective practitioner with strong parental engagement from most, she finds it very hard to build a rapport with some parents. She thinks there may be an issue about her nationality as they sometimes have conversations that she overhears, about supporting 'Brexit' and not being able to wait for the time when 'no more foreigners come in and take all our jobs and school places'.

continued

125

Whilst Marta treats parents in the same way, she finds the attitude of this group of parents to be a considerable challenge. Given the tensions here:

- **What can Marta do to improve the relationship?**

- **What should she avoid doing?**

- **Who else might she involve for support?**

- **What impact might this have on the children of this group of parents and how can she influence this?**

CASE STUDY 2

Narinder and Vijay Singh have one child, Anik. He was a premature, IVF baby who stayed in hospital for four weeks when he was born. He was one of triplets, and the only survivor.

Narinder is very protective of her son and comes to visit you more than once a week, checking that she has understood any messages in the home school diary, or telling you more about Anik's health issues so that you are aware. You feel conscious that this is affecting the amount of time that you can spend with other parents and you have observed that other children are noticing now much Narinder is talking to you. Anik is a delicate child who is discouraged from playing any 'rough' games in the playground by his parents.

- **How do you, as his class teacher/key person, manage the frequent visits?**

- **How do you head off any potential bullying?**

- **How can you support Narinder in the time available?**

Sharing observations and assessments for transition

As you know, the EYFS assesses children's development and progress from beginning to end, both informally and more formally. There are two points where a more formal capture of a child's development is made:

126

- the two-year-old check, which takes place at some time between a child's second and third birthdays;
- the final assessment, known as the Profile.

Many nurseries and childminders will not be producing the final profile, but they must ensure that information about a child's development against the early learning goals is transferred, as part of the transition process. This is an ideal time to review your paperwork, with the help of parents.

Longer activity: Assessment documentation

Think about how you share observation and information with parents and how they know how they can contribute to their children's development (Table 8.5).

TABLE 8.5 Assessment documentation

How do you currently share observations and assessments with parents?
What do you think works well?
Is there anything that could be improved?
What do parents think about it?
What changes will you make?

You may want to link this activity with the next one, which reviews transfer documentation. You might choose to start this off by working with the room leaders and/or senior management, or it might be a good opportunity to discuss how the process works and whether any changes are needed.

Longer activity: Transfer documentation review

Use your meetings to discuss the transfer documentation that you currently use.

Share with staff and parents, so you are all agreed on the effectiveness of the planning and paperwork. You might want to use the form in Table 8.6 as a basis for discussion and for recording any comments.

TABLE 8.6 Transfer documentation review: activity

Are all key members of staff aware of the transition to school policies?
How are school visits planned?
How do you communicate with schools?
How are parents consulted about the move to school?
Do teachers visit the settings?
How are children prepared for the transition?
Are children and their parents' views taken into account?
Action planning
Date:

School readiness

Numeracy and literacy – is this what *school readiness* is about?

The EYFS (DfE, 2017) requires practitioners to have 'a secure knowledge of early childhood development and how that leads to successful learning and development at school' (Standard 3.1). There is also a standard requiring practitioners to have knowledge of systematic synthetic phonics (3.4) and strategies to teach early maths (3.5).

Most importantly, 3.3 requires practitioners to:

> Demonstrate a critical understanding of the EYFS areas of learning and development and engage with the educational continuum of expectations, curricula and teaching of Key Stage 1 and 2.

As previously noted, we see from the characteristics of effective teaching and learning that the EYFS has an overarching responsibility to ensure that children learn *how to* learn, through the use of:

- playing and exploring;
- active learning;
- creating and thinking critically.

Whilst the setting will still be maintaining this focus, there are nonetheless frequent references in the press and media about the notion of 'school readiness'. This is a challenging term to unpick and may mean different things to different people. Whilst some might understand this to be about academic expectations, it might be that there is far more concern that a child develops enough confidence and independence to know that they can ask where the toilets are or where they can find their lunchbox than whether they can decode a word. The transition to a school environment, with new buildings, older children, larger playgrounds, different noises, smells, individuals, can be a cause of anxiety for families and familiarisation can be a significant factor in ensuring that a child is school ready.

The term 'school readiness' has been used by politicians and policymakers (Allen, 2011; Field, 2010; Tickell, 2011) but there is no one definition agreed by all. Most recently, the *Bold Beginnings* document, written about the importance of the reception year leading into the EYFSP (profile), noted that there is a general recognition that the Reception Year marks the onset of more formal teaching (Ofsted, 2017). The implication of this might be that reception is the transition year that moves away from play-based learning and prepares children for the expectations of learning within the National Curriculum.

This is a good opportunity for you to return to the overnight reflection and discuss school readiness.

🕐 Longer activity: What does school readiness mean to you?

Discuss: What does school readiness mean to you and your colleagues? Try to unpick this statement so that it relates to what you do. Then, think about what you need to relay to parents in terms of moving to school. Use post-it© notes to write down your thoughts.

Complete the same activity with parents (either ask them in a newsletter or email a message to them) so you have a good idea what they think. This is something that you can complete and share with parents at the beginning of their time in the pre-school room.

You can then use the diamond 9 sheet (see downloadable resources for Chapter 9) to categorise your post-it© notes and discuss the importance of various factors.

Whatever your conclusion about the meaning of school readiness, there is no doubt that supporting emergent literacy and numeracy needs to play a part in children's development and this can be done both at the setting and at home. In Feiler *et al.*'s book (2007), the ideas on activities include children and practitioners making a video to show parents examples of everyday literacy and numeracy, then encouraging parents and children to do the same at home. With so many smartphones that can easily take good videos, this is something that many families can complete with no additional cost.

School readiness is important for parents as well as children

The management of this particular transition has an element of the unknown about it, as a child may be transferring to an unknown school, even an unknown area.

> Little is known about the various ways in which parents become involved, or about different strategies that teachers use to promote parent involvement in prior-to-school settings. However, previous research has suggested that parent involvement patterns change when children make the transition from prior-to-school settings to school.'
>
> (Murray, McFarland-Piazza & Harrison, 2015, p. 1034)

In this paper, the authors explore the differences between pre-school and school engagement with parents and cite American research that notes that the frequency and direction of travel of parent/practitioner to parent/teacher contact is a) likely to be more frequent in pre-school settings and b) more likely to be initiated by parents than teachers (Rimm-Kaufman & Pianta, 1999). So what does this mean, 20 years later and in the UK?

As with any research, the findings on one paper cannot be seen as definitive evidence that certain practices take place as a rule. However, there are sufficient indicators in a number of studies that suggest that the relationships between teachers and parents are of a different style to those of early years practitioners and parents (Rimm-Kaufman & Pianta, 1999; Shields, 2009; Yeboah, 2002). In this context there is a responsibility upon early years practitioners to strive to maintain parents' confidence in engaging with school staff and also to manage the expectations of parents as they enter a new environment. You will find more information on transitions in Chapter 5.

Factors affecting successful transition to school

Yeboah (2002, p. 55) notes the following aspects have an impact on the transition to school:

- learning in different settings;
- factors associated with the school;
- factors associated with the home;
- factors associated with language and culture;
- the child's personal factors and characteristics.

Longer activity: Transition to school

Taking the above factors, discuss what each of them exactly means and identify some examples that could affect transitions (Table 8.7, p. 134). Each group could take one area.

Once practitioners have completed Table 8.7, choose some of the examples given and discuss how parents and children can be prepared to manage this element of change.

Building trusting relationships in pre-school can pay dividends in other settings

The involvement of parents in a pre-school setting can make all the difference to the transition from pre-school to school, as knowledge sharing can take place between practitioners but also between parents, so in this phase it is vitally important that parents start to engage – before they move to the school. Early years settings can also

TABLE 8.7 Transition to school: activity

Think of any examples	Learning in different settings	Factors associated with the school	Factors associated with the home	Factors associated with language and culture	The child's personal factors and characteristics
Example	Different teaching styles, different faces	Children have to wear a school uniform	There may be an older sister already attending the school	English is not the first language	The child may be very outgoing and find change easy to manage

model best practice in parental involvement so parents who are less confident have already had experience in building trusting relationships and understand how much their engagement with the settings is valued.

Saying goodbye

What to arrange

There are two factors to consider when children move on: robust preparation for the next experience that they are going to have and awareness that the attachments formed in the setting they are in will result in some sadness at leaving (for all involved).

There are many ways of celebrating the time children have spent in a setting, from a 'graduation', with gowns, ceremony and leaving certificate to the giving of a card or a small memento of the setting. By looking online, you will find many ideas of different ways to celebrate, including:

- days out;
- picnics;
- the giving of gifts, such as setting t-shirts, books, cuddly toys;
- ceremonies and awards.

Short activity

TABLE 8.8 Celebrating children's achievements: activity

How do you celebrate children's achievements before they leave?	
What are the pros and cons of what you do?	
Do all parents engage in it?	
Have parents been consulted about it?	
What else could you consider?	

There are factors that might make you reluctant to ask parents what they would like to do, mainly revolving around cost – both for parents and for the setting. However, you could discuss feasible options (Table 8.8) and then put a number of these to the parents and ask for their feedback.

Have you already asked parents what skills they have that you could use to support a venture such as a filming project? You may find a number of parents have strong technical skills and could become involved in editing a short film. Not only would that save money, but also it could establish links (with dads and possibly wider family too, and offer parents a role of expertise within the setting).

Confidence building in order that parents are assertive in the next setting

One useful goal for all settings is that parents and children move into the next setting having learned that their input is valued and is used to promote children's learning and development. It is also important that children believe in their own capabilities in terms of literacy, as research indicates the 'importance of self-assurance in relation to learning' (Feiler, 2005, p. 138). Feiler talks about the disadvantages that some children experience as a result of their socio-economic status, and goes on to say how important the home learning environment is. By offering parents opportunities to participate in their children's learning, they are less likely to be thwarted if, as Feiler states, 'there is a pervasive uni-directionality in school/home links' (2005, p. 133).

A number of papers (Crozier, 2006; Murray *et al.*, 2015) reflect in some way Polly Shield's assertion that, 'Most parents felt that they had a more distant and less reciprocal relationship with their child's teacher than they had with their key worker at nursery.' (Shields, 2009, p. 237). Therefore, it is important to manage the expectations of parents as well as encourage them to have a strong sense of their own value in terms of their child's education.

Longer activity

Using the principles of strength-based practice (see Chapter 3), design cards for parents, thanking them for their contributions and giving examples of when you particularly valued their engagement.

RESOURCES **TABLE 8.9** Practice review

Chapter section	Fully engaged with strategies in place	Somewhat engaged	Further development needed
What's happening in the pre-school phase			
Developing dialogues with parents			
Sharing observation and assessments			
School readiness			
Saying goodbye			
Reflection on chapter			
What changes have you made?			
What needs further development?			

References

Allen, G. (2011). *Early intervention: the next steps: An independent report to Her Majesty's Government*. London: HM Government.

Crozier, G. (2006). Parents and schools: partnership or surveillance? *Journal of Education Policy, 13* (1), 125–136.

Department for Education (DfE). (2017). *Statutory Framework for the Early Years Foundation Stage*. London: DfE.

Early Education. (2012). *Development Matters*. www.early-education.org.uk.

Erdreich, L. & Golden, D. (2016). The cultural shaping of parental involvement: Theoretical insights from Israeli Jewish parents' involvement in the primary schooling of their children. *International Studies in Sociology of Education, 26* (1), 51–65.

Feiler, A. (2005). Linking home and school literacy in an inner city reception class. *Journal of Early Childhood Literacy, 5* (2), 131–149.

Feiler, A., Andrews, J., Greenhough, P., Hughes, M., Scanlan, M., & Wan Ching Yee with Johnson, D. (2007). *Improving primary literacy: Linking home and school*. London: Routledge.

Field, F. (2010). *The foundation years: Preventing poor children becoming poor adults: The report of the independent review on poverty and life chances*. London: HM Government.

Lareau, A. (1987). Social class differences in family–school relationships: The importance of cultural capital. *Sociology of Education, 60*, 73–85.

Murray, E., McFarland-Piazza, L. & Harrison, L.J. (2015). Changing patterns of parent–teacher communication and parent involvement from preschool to school. *Early Child Development and Care, 185* (7), 1031–1052.

National College for Teaching and Leadership (NCTL) (2013). *Teachers' standards (early years)*. Retrieved from: https://www.gov.uk/government/uploads/system/uploads/attachment_data/file/211646/Early_Years_Teachers__Standards.pdf

Office for Standards in Education (Ofsted) (2018). *Early years inspection handbook*. London: Ofsted.

Ofsted (2017). *Bold beginnings: The reception curriculum in a sample of good and outstanding primary schools*. London: Ofsted.

Rimm-Kaufman, S.E. & Pianta, R.C. (1999). Patterns of family–school contact in preschool and kindergarten. *School Psychology Review, 28* (3), 426–438.

Shields, P. (2009). 'School doesn't feel as much of a partnership': Parents' perceptions of their children's transitions from nursery school to reception class. *Early Years, 29* (3), 237–248.

Tickell, C. (2011). *The early years: Foundations for life, health and learning*. London: Department for Education.

Yeboah, D.A. (2002) Enhancing transition from early childhood phase to primary education: Evidence from the research literature. *Early Years, 22* (1), 51–68.

9 Creating a parent-friendly environment

TABLE 9.1 Links to EY documentation

Teachers' Standards (Early Years), (NCTL, 2013)	Early years inspection handbook (Ofsted, updated 2018)	*Statutory framework for early years foundation stage (DfE, 2017)*
2.7 8.1 8.2 8.6	s. 151 (p. 31) s. 160 (p. 40)	s. 3.61 (p. 30) s. 3.68 (p. 31)

This chapter looks at the range of ways, across the age groups, that settings can ensure that parents have an investment in an environment in which they feel they play a part. It will allow setting managers to audit the ways that parents are involved and uses case study to illustrate good practice in settings that draws in not just mothers and fathers but wider family members who may have more time to offer the setting.

Overnight reflection

What does a parent-friendly environment mean to you? Think about what you mean by this, and think of three or four elements of any environment that make it feel friendly and safe (Table 9.2). Be ready to discuss this in your training sessions.

- The importance of the environment
- Privacy and partnership
- A sense of belonging
- Support and information
- The importance of the environment (2)

TABLE 9.2 Practice reflection

Chapter section	Fully engaged with strategies in place	Somewhat engaged	Further development needed
Importance of the environment			
Privacy and partnership			
A sense of belonging			
Support and information			
What strategies are currently in place?			
What needs further development?			

The aspects of the environment listed on page 140 will influence parents' sense of belonging and identity and make them feel that they are part of the setting. Consider the quote below as you start to reflect upon the ways in which parents in your setting are involved:

QUOTE FOR DISCUSSION OR REFLECTION

First, opportunities for involvement should be accessible for families, rather than cumbersome. Secondly, a viable set of supports should be in place to encourage parent involvement. Finally, various involvement opportunities should exist that allow families to use their strengths and talents.
(Murray, McFarland-Piazza & Harrison, 2015, pp. 1033–1034)

In this chapter and the next, the focus will be on creating ways to make parents feel more involved. This chapter will prioritise the creation of a welcoming space that feels as much as possible like a home from home for parents as well as children. In Chapter 10, we shall be looking at the ways to communicate with parents in order to maximise opportunities for engagement. You could think of this as a review of practice, firstly looking inwardly at what parents experience as they come to the setting, then looking at the connections from setting to parents that can help to engage parents and give them support and confidence.

The importance of the environment

You might have been thinking for some time that your setting is in need of some attention, but with time pressures as they are, this type of long-term, costly, non-urgent task can often be parked while more urgent matters are pressing. However, this could be a valuable commercial decision in that it might attract more families to use your services. Use this training time as an opportunity to get feedback from the staff and parents too – what, if anything, is missing that might make for a more positive environment for all participants?

You can start where you like but this activity will start with the entrance hall as this is where first impressions are gained.

Longer activity: Entrance hall review

Before the session starts, the training lead should take some photos of the entrance hall to your setting. Print them out and give a set to practitioners who should work in groups of three or four.

Discuss: how does this appear to parents? Imagine you are a new parent coming in – what does your eye get drawn towards? Think about colour, language, nursery branding, congestion etc.

Use Table 9.3 (p. 140) to capture your thoughts.

You can repeat this exercise in all of the rooms, in the hall, or any area where parents are likely to be. It may be that you have never looked at the space with the perspective of a parent, and perhaps not thought about what parents might find useful.

This activity may have given you a sense of what might be important in an environment, through thinking about quite practical aspects such as décor and signage, and the next activity looks at what the most important aspects of a parent-friendly environment really are. Both activities can be completed with your staff but may also be something to complete in a parents' meeting. This joint engagement is a good way to demonstrate that parents are valued and it is another opportunity to engage with them and get their views. It is, however, inevitable that there will be a number of different views resulting in you not being able to please everyone, so having a rationale for your final choices will ensure a fair playing field.

TABLE 9.3 Environmental review: activity

Review of entrance	Pros	Cons
Colour/decor		
Language/s		
Space		
Branding/signage		
Other		
Plans for change?		

Environment

It is important to unpick the term environment as it can mean a whole range of things. Having thought about what is important in a parent-friendly environment, let's just think about what we include in the term 'environment'? Is it rooms and objects? Is it atmosphere? Is it people? Is it wider than the setting, for example, is it the neighbourhood? Is it indoors, outdoors, both? Beyond the setting? Local parks and playgrounds that the children visit?

Diamond 9 activities

A useful tool for discussion is the diamond 9 diagram (Figure 9.1). You will find a photocopiable version within the e-resources for this book. It is a useful way of prioritising and discussing a range of issues and helps to structure and direct conversations.

⚡ Short activity: Diamond 9

What are most important aspects of a parent-friendly environment?

In groups, ask practitioners to rank the phrases in Figure 9.2 in terms of helping to create a parent-friendly environment, using the diamond 9 template (Figure 9.1). Before the activity starts, cut out the phrases (Figure 9.2) and laminate a set for each group. You can add other phrases that you think are relevant to your setting. There are more than nine phrases here so teams will have to reject some of the phrases and choose the ones most important to them. You can also give them some blank pieces of paper in case they want to add some of their own – no more than three. Encourage practitioners to take their time with this.

⚡ Short activity: Diamond 9 extension

When groups have completed this, ask them to compare their priorities and discuss their views.

- Did people find it hard to agree or was there some consensus?
- How did the 'practical' features (clean, tidy) compare with the atmospheric ones, or the organisational ones?
- Did the groups have similar patterns?

For future activities, you can use different combinations of the phrases to see how the direction of the conversation changes.

The next activity maintains the moving around of laminated words, but this time looking at your setting's environment in particular, with strengths and areas for development.

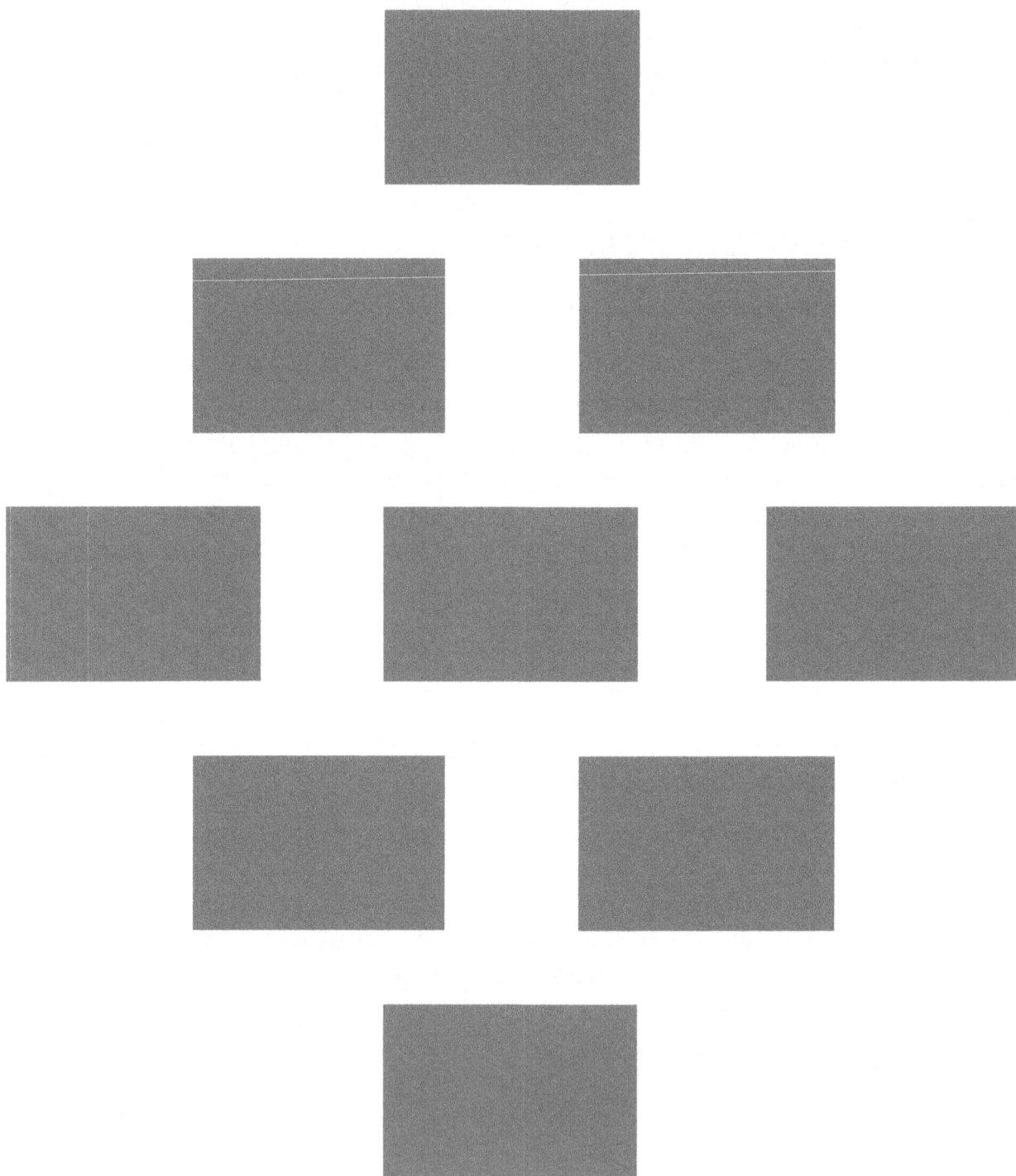

FIGURE 9.1 Activity diamond

Clean and freshly decorated	
Tidy and ordered	Opportunities for sharing ideas
Friendly staff who know all the parents	Opportunities for meeting other parents
Trusting relationships	Friendly and inclusive atmosphere
Shared perspectives	Opportunities for all the family to be involved
Space for discussion	Health and safety in place
Privacy for discussion	Sense of belonging
Wide range of communication between parents and practitioners	Provision of useful information (e.g. local cultural support; benefits information) for families

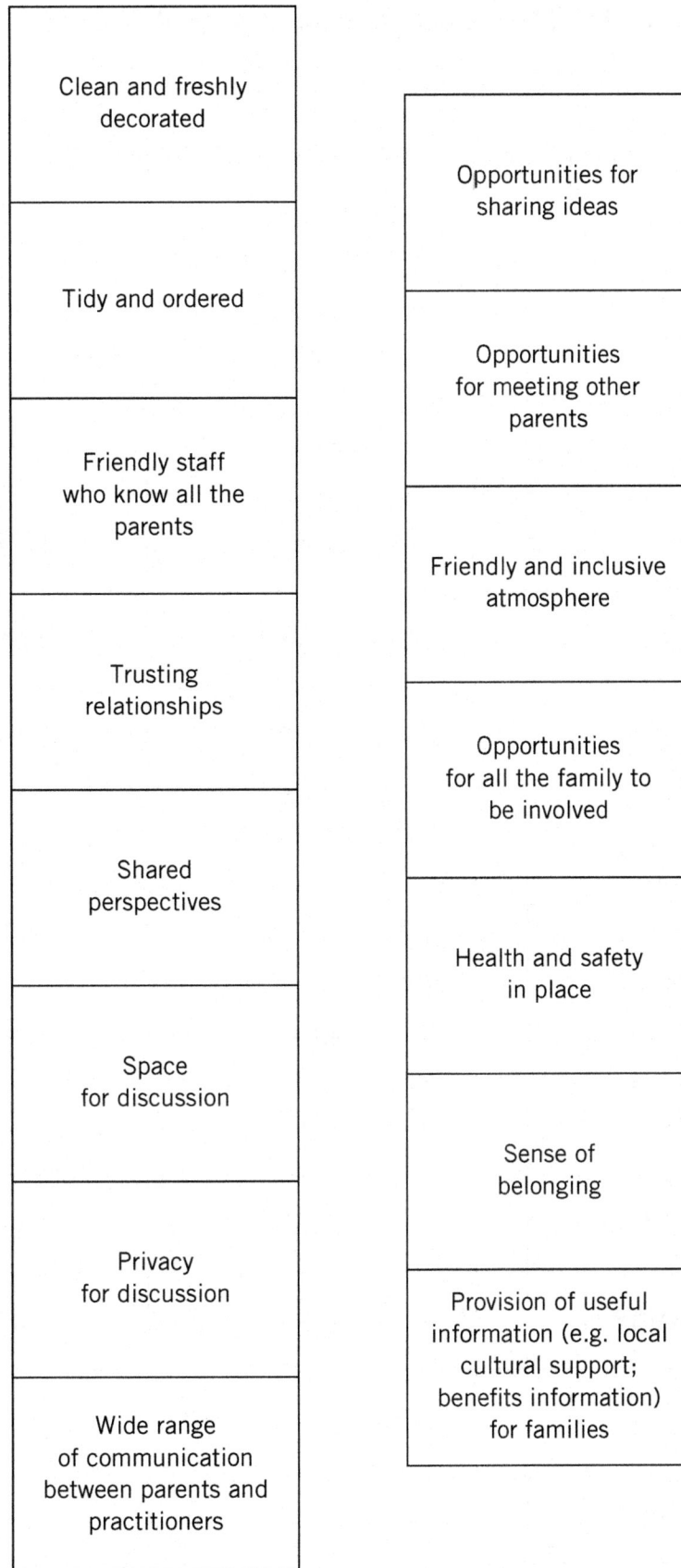

FIGURE 9.2 What makes a parent-friendly environment?

Longer activity: Describing your environment

What words would you use to describe the environment in your setting?

Use these words by cutting them out and laminating them:

busy	happy	chatty
toxic	playful	friendly
stressful	active	bureaucratic
inclusive	organised	welcoming
informative	child-friendly	parent-friendly
safe	competitive	strict
open	attractive	modern
clean	bright	austere
colourful	hierarchical	tidy
structured	smelly	positive
collaborative	tense	negative

You can add more words of your own.

Some of these words can have both negative and positive interpretations so they won't mean the same to everyone. Discuss them from a parent-centred lens – how does the environment in the setting work for them?

In groups, agree the three top positive words that relate to the atmosphere in the setting. Then do the same for challenging aspects – what areas do you think the setting needs to consider in terms of developing strategies? So now you have three words representing the strengths of the atmosphere of the setting and three representing the negative aspects. The atmosphere and environment that you work in, and the tone of it, will be apparent to parents when they come in and out of the setting.

If you are doing this in groups, how do the words chosen by the groups compare? Leave the words as they are for a while – you have chosen three + and three –. Now the focus will be on other aspects of a parent-friendly environment.

Partnership and privacy

Partnerships with parents can flourish when communication is at its most effective. In order to do this, there should be places to talk. In reality, this may be one of the following:

- entrance
- manager's office
- corridor
- children's rooms.

Think about the places that you hold your conversations with parents. Some parents will tell anecdotes about the only time they are invited to talk to a teacher/practitioner is when their child is in trouble! Do you ensure that you talk to parents on a regular basis, and if so, is there somewhere private that you can talk? There is a requirement in the *Statutory Framework for the EYFS* to provide an area where staff and parents can talk confidentially (DfE, 2017, p. 30) but this may require booking and planning. How do you manage when a parent needs to talk to you at short notice and what could be a solution?

🕐 Longer activity: Where do you talk to parents?

Communication in a private – and comfortable if possible – location means that practitioners and parents can build relationships through sharing confidential information. This excerpt from a publication considers how the relationship between parents and practitioners can change according to the environment. Share with the team:

Nursery 3 was physically structured in such a way that it was difficult for adults to get beyond the entrance area, so children tended to be dropped off and collected at this point. This only allowed for brief exchanges of information.

In nurseries 1 and 2 the physical environment was much more conducive to parents staying and participating, with comfortable sofas where parents could chat informally with other parents and staff over a cup of coffee. In this setting there were many more opportunities for sharing information and parents felt there was less 'distance' between them and the staff, which in turn made it easier for them to ask for advice:

> I just like her, I like all of them, they're all nice, they're so friendly and they can chat away to you, like I say not like teacher and mother, it's just friends, everybody's just friends.

Practitioners at these two nurseries also emphasised the importance of having friendships with parents and creating an environment in which they could meet in a relaxed and informal manner:

> Well in the family rooms we encourage them to sit about and we have a coffee, you know, stay as long as you like . . .

> It's taking time out to spend, to chat to the parents . . . and it gets to be like friendships.

> We're not staff, we have parents nights out and things and you make the effort, even if you don't really want to go you make the effort to show them that you're part of them . . . to break the barriers down.

(Riddick & Hall, 2000, pp. 125–126)

Download and print the quotation for practitioners to read and discuss in groups.

- Do you see any of this practice reflected in your own setting? If so, which parts?
- What do you think about the staff comments? Is there anything that you particularly agree with or think you would not do?
- Discuss which nurseries are likely to have the most effective partnerships working.
- What do you think about the final paragraph and the boundaries in the setting?
- Would you suggest any changes to your setting's practice in the light of your discussions?

Use the quotations to reflect upon the places where you talk to parents. Does it tend to be in the entrance space because space is at such a premium that there is often someone else in the office and children/other practitioners in the rooms? Often, the corridor is the most private place in the building. Perhaps it doesn't matter where the conversation takes place if the relationship is positive, but if a new parent needs to speak to their key person about a personal issue, it might be a barrier and the parent might decide not to speak.

A sense of belonging

The barriers to strong parent–practitioner partnerships are sometimes rooted in parents feeling that they are not valued in the setting; that they are the less-knowledgeable member of the 'partnership' (Hoover-Dempsey *et al.*, 2005). Sometimes you may hear about practitioners using an 'expert' model of practice (Davis *et al.*, 2002) whereby the practitioners adopt the role of experts and the parents are there to learn from them. The partnership model of working with parents involves sharing knowledge and working together. There are ways of doing this, which might include inviting parents to share information at various events and through different means of communication (see Chapter 10). Nevertheless, just as you work to make children feel at home in this new environment, how do you do the same for parents, and what benefits might you gain by doing so.

This is not just about pictures on the wall, but also about interests (shared interest in the child); about local community activities; about the people in the setting having a shared identity: how do you achieve that?

Longer activity: A sense of belonging

Work in pairs and identify some activity/intervention that may give parents a stronger sense of belonging (Table 9.4). It could be setting up a buddying system whereby all new parents have a parent contact who is already in the setting. Think about the planning that is needed (you will need to be sure that you have enough parents to agree to do this, and you have to consider how they will contact each other) and when you might be able to implement this. Once all the pairs have had a chance to make a suggestion, agree which ones you want to take forward, and then put those ones to the parents in the setting.

TABLE 9.4 A sense of belonging: activity

Building a sense of belonging activities	Do we do it already?	What planning would it require?	When could it be implemented
Buddy system	No	Volunteer parents; meeting room for discussion; permission to share contact details	Within one month?
Parents invited regularly to the setting	Yes, but not many come because they are all at work	We need to think about finding more convenient times for them to come	Might take longer ...

Support and information

One of the opportunities of working with parents is the chance to support parents who need some kind of additional information or signposting. This could be something like help with English or benefits information, but it could also be the opportunity to give parents help with parenting their child. Through the trusting relationship, brought about through thought, empathy and engagement, new opportunities to help parents and therefore children can grow, as 'parents who wish to disclose concerns are generally drawn to certain favoured settings and professionals and these settings can be critical conduits for early identification and referral' (Brown *et al.*, 2012, p. 41). Parents are more likely to share concerns if they feel that they belong and that they can trust the professionals they are working with. The supply of relevant information that is available for parents to take away, plus a good knowledge of both local and national services will ensure the provision of relevant materials.

Longer activity: Sharing information

Undertake a review of relevant information that could be shared with parents. Bear in mind that parents might be interested in some information but do not want to share publicly that they are interested (e.g. adult literacy classes). How do you know what parents are interested in? How is the information shared? Do people know it is there? For this activity, there might be three elements:

- What are we currently sharing?
- What do parents want?
- What do practitioners know about that they can share?

In your meeting, discuss the best ways of gathering the information from these three points. For example, you could check on the materials available – are they all still current?

The importance of the environment (2)

Now that you have had a chance to reflect on particular aspects of the parent–practitioner partnership and how the environment can affect it for the better or worse, go back to the three positive and three developmental words that you identified earlier on in this chapter. Think about whether you can improve upon the positives and make changes to eliminate the negatives (Table 9.5).

TABLE 9.5 Improvement plan

Positives	Improvement plan?
1	
2	
3	

Negatives	How can we move away from these?
1	
2	
3	

Finally, this chapter is about the creation of a positive environment. Celebrate your achievements by reflecting back and recognising what you do (Table 9.6).

References

Brown, E.R., Khan, L. & Parsonage, M. (2012). *A chance to change: Delivering effective parenting programmes to change lives.* London: Centre for Mental Health. Available at: www.centreformentalhealth.org.uk/publications/chance_to_change.aspx

Davis, H., Day, C. & Bidmead, C. (2002). *Working in partnership with parents.* London: Pearson.

Department for Education (DfE) (2017). *Statutory framework for the early years foundation stage.* London: DfE.

Hoover Dempsey, K.V., Walker, J.M.T., Sandler, H.M., Whetsel, D., Green, C.L., Wilkins, A.S. & Closson, K. (2005). Why do parents become involved? Research findings and implications. *The Elementary School Journal*, 106 (2), 105–130.

Murray, E., McFarland-Piazza, L. & Harrison, L.J. (2015). Changing patterns of parent–teacher communication and parent involvement from preschool to school. *Early Child Development and Care*, 185 (7), 1031–1052.

National College for Teaching and Leadership (NCTL) (2013). *Teachers' standards (early years).* Retrieved from: https://www.gov.uk/government/uploads/system/uploads/attachment_data/file/211646/Early_Years_Teachers__Standards.pdf

TABLE 9.6 Practice review

Chapter section	Fully engaged with strategies in place	Somewhat engaged	Further development needed
Importance of the environment			
Privacy and partnership			
A sense of belonging			
Support and information			
Reflection on chapter			
What changes have you made?			
What needs further development?			

Office for Standards in Education (Ofsted) (2018). *Early years inspection handbook*. London: Ofsted.

Riddick, B. & Hall, E. (2000). Match or Mismatch: The perceptions of parents of nursery age children related to those of the children's main nursery workers. *International Journal of Early Years Education, 8* (2), 113–128.

10 Communication between parents and settings

Sharing children's development and progress

TABLE 10.1 Links to EY documentation

Teachers' Standards (Early Years), (NCTL, 2013)	Early years inspection handbook (Ofsted, updated 2018)	*Statutory framework for early years foundation stage (DfE, 2017)*
4.3 5.5 6.3	s. 156 (p. 37) s. 160 (p. 40)	s. 1.6 (p. 9) s. 1.10 (p. 10) s. 2.2 (p. 13) s. 2.9 (p. 14) s. 3.3 (p. 16) s. 3.28 (p. 23) s. 3.44 and 3.46 (p. 27) s. 3.47 and 3.50 (p. 28) s. 3.52 (p. 28) s. 3.68 and 3.73 (p. 32) s. 3.74 and 3.75 (p. 33)

Building on the activities from the previous chapter, this chapter will consider both face-to-face and other opportunities to connect with parents. It will look at the purposes of staying in touch and consider the setting-specific opportunities and challenges to develop in practice. Very often, some reflection upon communication skills can make a difference to the messages exchanged. Communication with parents can sometimes prove challenging for a variety of reasons, including professional commitments, time, cultural assumptions, social unease, literacy or numeracy issues. This chapter will therefore encourage settings to explore how they can reach all parents and carers so that the importance of the home learning environment and the benefits of parental engagement can be celebrated. The key aspect of this chapter is to consider the ways that those parents who do not engage in regular communication can feel part of the process of helping their child to learn and play.

- Hows and whys of communication with parents
- EYFS *Statutory Framework* (DfE, 2017) communication requirements
- Once you know how and why you communicate, what else is there to know?
- Exploring common interests and backgrounds

TABLE 10.2 Practice reflection

Chapter section	Fully engaged with strategies in place	Somewhat engaged	Further development needed
Hows and whys of communication with parents			
EYFS: communication requirements			
Practical communication			
Reading expressions			
What strategies are currently in place?			
What needs further development?			

Overnight reflection

What is your preferred method of staying in touch with parents and families? What are the reasons for your preference? Take a while to consider the most effective method that you use to stay in touch with parents and what you like about it. Think about that method of communication as a whole: are there little glitches that you would like to improve upon? Do parents like it as much as you do? Are there some parents who do not engage with it at all? What can you do to remedy this?

Staying in touch with families

First, it is important to consider why we stay in touch with families. It is only by reflecting on the wider importance of regular contact that it is possible to cross barriers and continually review the ways of making contact and adapt it to the families that are involved in the setting at any given time.

Short activity

Spend some time thinking about the reasons why practitioners make efforts to maintain regular contact with parents (use Figure 10.1). Are the reasons all connected to children's development and learning or could there be other reasons? Think about the benefits to all involved: children, parents themselves and your own setting.

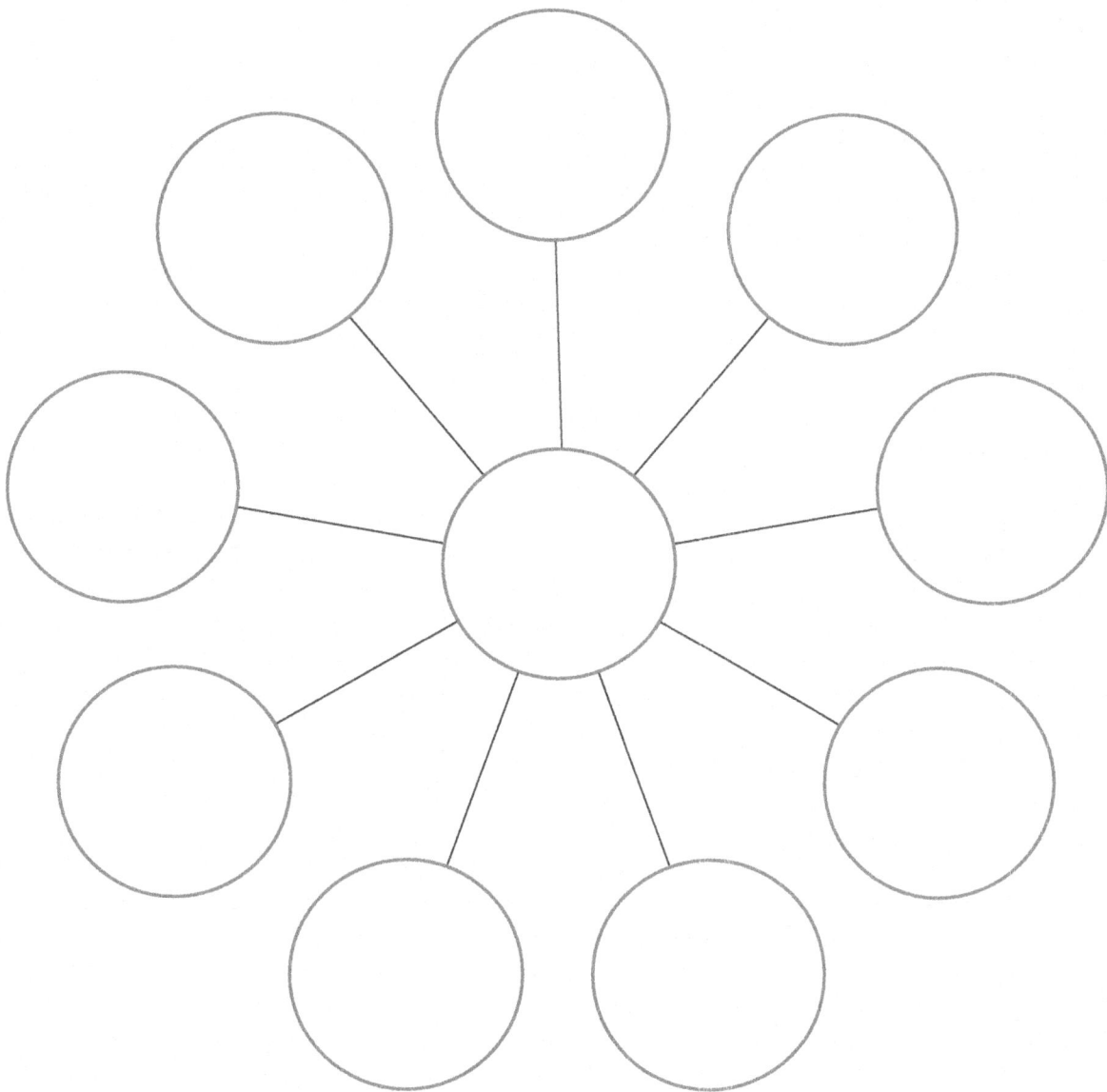

FIGURE 10.1 Why stay in touch with families (1)?

You might get something like this (Figure 10.2).

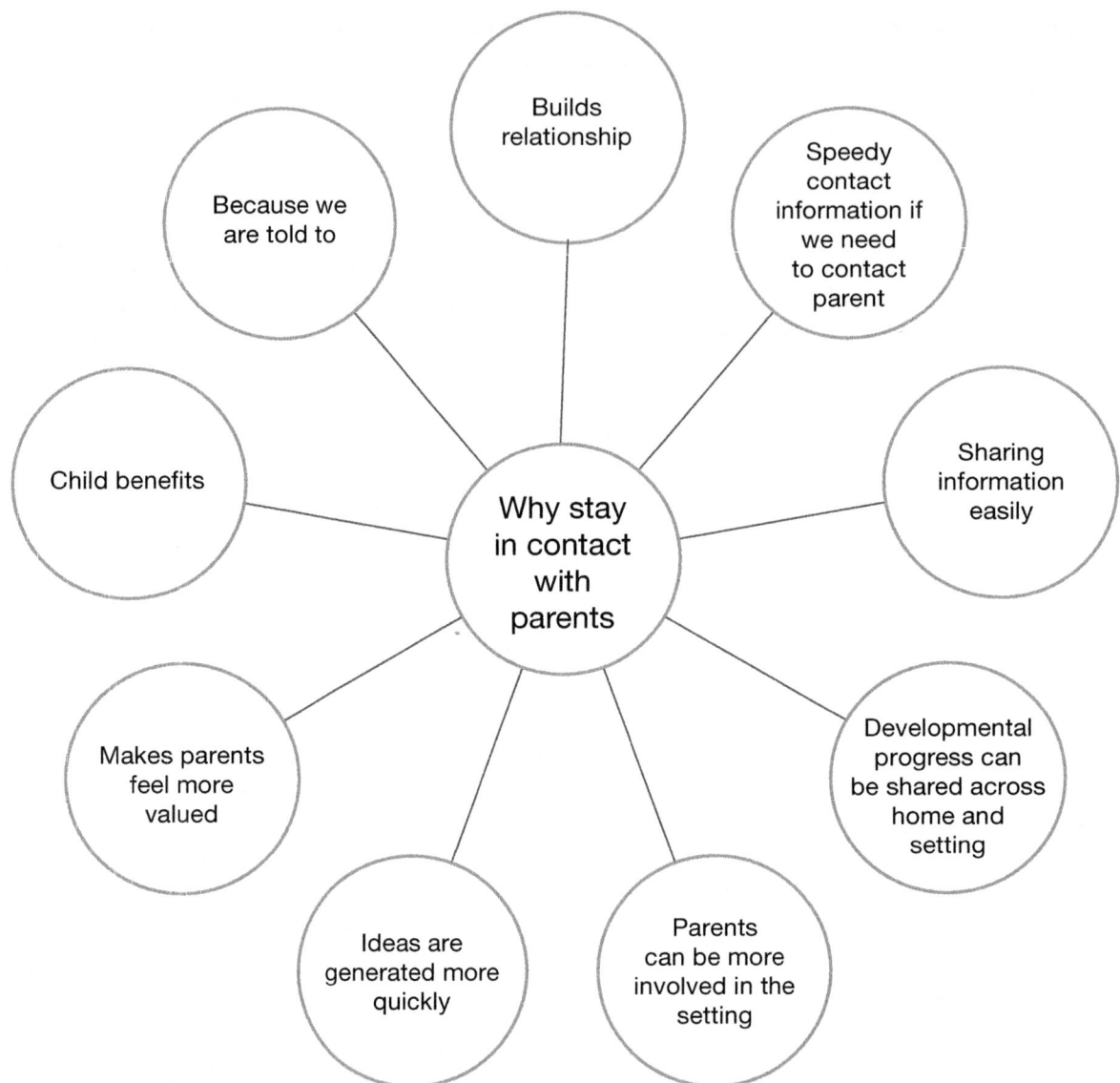

FIGURE 10.2 Why stay in touch with families (2)?

Add the missing ones onto your sphere if they are not there already.

Here is a sample of quotes from papers that have explored the benefits of partnership with parents in terms of children's outcomes – you might want to laminate it and put it on the wall to motivate practitioners and show parents how much you value them.

QUOTES FOR REFLECTION OR DISCUSSION

Evidence-base of working with parents

The most important finding from the point of view of this review is that parental involvement in the form of 'at home good parenting' has a significant positive effect on children's achievement and adjustment even after all other factors shaping attainment have been taken out of the equation. . . . The scale of the impact is evident across all social classes and all ethnic groups.

(Desforges & Abouchaar, 2003, p. 5)

The more engaged parents are in the education of their children the more likely their children are to succeed in the education system. School improvement and school effectiveness research consistently shows that parental engagement is one of the key factors in securing higher student achievement. Schools that improve and sustain improvement engage the community and build strong links with parents. Where schools build positive relationships with parents and work actively to embrace racial, religious, and ethnic and language differences, evidence of sustained school improvement can be found.

(Goodall & Vorhaus, 2010, p. 3)

There are many reasons for developing school, family, and community partnerships. They can improve school programs and school climate, provide family services and support, increase parents' skills and leadership, connect families with others in the school and in the community, and help teachers with their work. However, the main reason to create such partnerships is to help all youngsters succeed in school and in later life. When parents, teachers, students, and others view one another as partners in education, a caring community forms around students and begins its work.

(Epstein, 1995, pp. 81–82)

The analyses confirm that parental involvement in activities (such as reading to their child, teaching songs and nursery rhymes, playing with letters &

continued

157

numbers, visiting the library, painting & drawing, emphasising the alphabet, etc.) are significant in accounting for differences in social/behavioural development at the start of primary school.

(Sylva, *et al.*, 2004, p. 29)

Parents are important in children's educational achievement.

(Meehan & Meehan, 2017, p. 3)

Parents' influence is important throughout childhood and adolescence.

(DfES, 2007, p. 5)

There is clearly significant public interest in making it as easy as possible for parents – fathers and mothers – to engage as partners in their children's learning and development from the earliest age.

(DfES, 2007, p. 6)

Short activity: Discussion

Next, use a large piece of flip chart paper and some post-it© notes, divided into sections, to reflect how you stay in contact with parents as a setting. If you have a larger group, you could ask each group to take a category and think of everything that is communicated in that way:

- face to face;
- online (Facebook page; twitter; texting, online learning journal or similar);
- written to individual (either through email, post or in child's bag);
- written to groups (either through email, post or in child's bag);
- telephone.

Keep this sheet of paper on the wall – you will be coming back to it.

Now you have completed your audit of all the methods of communication that you use, look at the sheet.

- Are there any segments that do not look as full as the others? Why do you think that is?
- You will probably have many of the following on your diagram in Figure 10.2.
  - outings
  - new setting visits
  - attendance

- complaints
- behaviour issue (small)
- behaviour issue (ongoing)
- behaviour issues (significant)
- explaining policies and procedures
- staff deployment – allocation of a key person
- concerns about something the child has said
- transition planning
- fundraising
- developmental meetings
- parents' evenings
- and more besides.

Longer activity: Communication methods

So the question is, how would you communicate the above, and why would you use that method?

Discuss in your groups. If there are some disagreements, bring them to the main group at the end of the activity. It can be easy to continue with one method of communication when it is not necessarily the way that will guarantee the widest engagement, so spend time reflecting on practice.

At the end of this activity, make an action plan to implement any changes in types of communication.

In a survey exploring this (Wilson, 2016), practitioners were asked about the methods used to maintain links with parents. Table 10.3 shows the responses of different methods in a range of settings:

Short activity

You can see from Table 10.3 that the least used methods of communication are the online ones. Why do you think that is? Do you use them in your setting? What do you think parents would think of them? Would it help those who are less able to be present?

TABLE 10.3 Communication methods

Contact with settings	Practitioners (%)	Contact with settings	Practitioners (%)
Newsletters	89	Texts	35
Emailing	68	Children's activities supported across home and setting	59
Twitter	8	Facebook	9
Other social media platforms	6	Video links to settings	6
One to one meetings about child's development	64	Home visits	36
Informal conversations	43	Fundraising events	47
Invitations to setting activities	65	Invitations to participate at setting	57
Discussions on children's interests	45	Other	8

How are you communicating what you have to communicate?

There are a number of pieces of information in the EYFS Statutory Framework (DfE, 2017) that you are required to convey to parents (there are some variations in the method of communication in relation to childminders).

Longer activity: Maintaining records

Check that you are complying with this list and that you have records. Table 10.4 could be used for a record. You may have done some or all of this in Chapter 2, but look at it now with a more critical eye, checking that the message is conveyed effectively.

TABLE 10.4 Maintaining records

EYFS *Statutory Framework* requirements		
What it says:	**What we do now (date)**	**When this will be reviewed**
1.6 'if a child's progress in any prime area gives cause for concern, practitioners must discuss this with the child's parents and/or carers and agree how to support the child. Practitioners must consider whether a child may have a special educational need or disability which requires specialist support. They should link with, and help families to access, relevant services from other agencies as appropriate.'		
1.7 'If a child does not have a strong grasp of English language, practitioners must explore the child's skills in the home language with parents and/or carers, to establish whether there is cause for concern about language delay.'		
1.10 'Providers must inform parents and/or carers of the name of the key person, and explain their role, when a child starts attending a setting.'		
2.2 'Parents and/or carers should be kept up to date with their child's progress and development. Practitioners should address any learning and development needs in partnership with parents and/or carers, and any relevant professionals.'		
2.3, 2.4 and 2.5 'Practitioners must provide a short written summary of their child's development in the prime areas, and they should develop a targeted plan involving parents and other professionals if there are significant concerns.' 'Practitioners must discuss with parents and/or carers how the summary of development can be used to support learning at home.' 'Practitioners must agree with parents and/or carers when will be the most useful point to provide a summary.'		
2.9 'Schools must share the results of the Profile with parents and/or carers, and explain to them when and how they can discuss the Profile with the teacher/practitioner who completed it.'		
3.3 'Childminders are not required to have written policies and procedures. However, they must be able to explain their policies and procedures to parents, carers.'		
3.28 'Providers must inform parents and/or carers about staff deployment, and, when relevant and practical, aim to involve them in these decisions.'		
3.44 'The provider must promote the good health of children at tending the setting. They must have a procedure, discussed with parents and/or carers, for responding to children who are ill or infectious, take necessary steps to prevent the spread of infection, and take appropriate action if children are ill.'		

continued

TABLE 10.4 *continued*

EYFS *Statutory Framework* requirements		
What it says:	**What we do now (date)**	**When this will be reviewed**
3.46 'Medicine (both prescription and non-prescription) must only be administered to a child where written permission for that particular medicine has been obtained from the child's parent and/or carer. Providers must keep a written record each time a medicine is administered to a child, and inform the child's parents and/or carers on the same day, or as soon as reasonably practicable.'		
3.47 'Providers must record and act on information from parents and carers about a child's dietary needs.'		
3.50 'Providers must inform parents and/or carers of any accident or injury sustained by the child on the same day as, or as soon as reasonably practicable after, and of any first aid treatment given.'		
3.52 'Providers, including childminders, must keep a record of any occasion where physical intervention is used, and parents and/or carers must be informed on the same day, or as soon as reasonably practicable.'		
3.68 'Providers must maintain records and obtain and share information (with parents and carers, other professionals working with the child, the police, social services and Ofsted or the childminder agency with which they are registered, as appropriate) to ensure the safe and efficient management of the setting, and to help ensure the needs of all children are met. Providers must enable a regular two-way flow of information with parents and/or carers, and between providers, if a child is attending more than one setting. If requested, providers should incorporate parents' and/or carers' comments into children's records.'		
3.73 'Providers must make the following information available to parents and/or carers: • how the EYFS is being delivered in the setting . . . • the range and type of activities and experiences provided for children . . . • how the setting supports children with special educational needs and disabilities • food and drinks provided for children • details of the provider's policies and procedures . . . • staffing in the setting . . .' *Please see Table 2.4 on p. 23 for full version of this requirement.*		
3.74 'Providers must put in place a written procedure for dealing with concerns and complaints from parents and/or carers, and must keep a written record of any complaints, and their outcome.'		
3.75 'Providers must make available to parents and/or carers details about how to contact Ofsted or the childminder agency with which the provider is registered as appropriate, if they believe the provider is not meeting the EYFS requirements.'		

Once you know why and how you are communicating, what else is there to know?

The why and how of connecting with families are just the starting points of the process. There are many other factors in making this a successful enterprise, which include:

- listening skills;
- reading facial expressions;
- offering choices;
- being non-judgemental;
- showing empathy;
- being flexible.

Although it is often said that the power balance tends to be in favour of the practitioner, some, more inexperienced practitioners find working with parents quite challenging, especially when their assessments of a child's development is questioned (Brooker, 2010). Active listening is a skill that involves concentration and the ability to remove other distractions from the environment – this is not easy in a nursery or reception class! As well as listening actively, and focusing on what the parent is saying, it is important to treat this conversation very differently to the conversations you have at home with partners or friends. As a professional discussion, the bulleted aspects above should be brought into play, so you ensure that you are:

- paying attention to exactly what the person is saying;
- noticing whether their body language is revealing any unspoken concerns (e.g. through lack of eye contact, arms crossed over body);
- internally summarising what they are saying and considering the options that they might choose from (if appropriate) rather than only suggesting your preferred option;
- maintaining a neutral response and not giving your opinion, even if this topic may be something that you don't agree with (maybe to do with nutrition/weaning/behavioural issue);
- showing your understanding of their perspective through listening, paraphrasing what they have said, nodding, asking questions, demonstrating understanding through your body language;
- listening to their needs and trying to offer flexible responses. Sometimes parents cannot fit into the timings of the setting; look for ways to accommodate them. By offering flexibility, you might find that it repays benefits in kind at a later date.

How do you listen to different people?

When working with parents, your discussions (not all of them) might be different to those that you have with people in different relationships. Perhaps in your closest relationships, a lot goes 'unsaid', with no need to expand and you know what your family will want you to listen to. Do you reflect on the difference in structure between professional and personal conversation and the boundaries that you have to observe?

Short activity: Talking to different people

Think about the above and discuss in your groups (Table 10.5):

- family – parents – colleagues – friends

TABLE 10.5 Talking to different people: activity

What are the differences in the way you speak to people in those roles?
What are the principles behind the differences?
What are the most important factors to remember when listening to parents?

Reading facial expressions

Research has explored the shared understanding of basic facial expressions across cultures and communities for many years now; it is generally accepted that there is a common expression for the following 'six primary emotions – happy, surprise, fear, disgust-contempt, anger and sad.' (Jack, 2013, p. 7). Therefore, whatever the language spoken, it is likely that the facial expressions will be similar, regardless of culture, giving communities non-verbal information even when language barriers impede full understanding.

However, some recent research (Killgore *et al.*, 2017) also noted that when people are sleep deprived, it is more difficult to read subtler expressions of sadness and happiness. Therefore, when you are having a conversation bear in mind that tired parents may not be interpreting your body language as accurately as you might expect!

Short activity: Reading facial expressions

Divide the group into two teams, and cut out some pieces of paper with the words in Table 10.6.

TABLE 10.6 Reading facial expressions: activity

Disgust	Fear	Contempt	Joy
Anger	Sadness	Surprise	

Each team should agree an expression, and all demonstrate that expression (i.e., the group chooses 'joy' and then all try to express joy on their faces). The other team has to guess the expression and then takes a turn themselves. This continues until all the expressions have been completed by each group.

Building trust by exploring common interests and backgrounds

There are some elements about us that are explicit: our identified gender, ethnicity, our age and so on. But there are other factors that can build bridges with parents and result in a shared interest that might make parents feel more engaged with the setting (i.e. there are people like me here . . . I belong here).

Short activity: What do you have in common with your colleagues?

Five minutes in pairs with someone you do not usually work with – open questions; using cues and listening skills (nodding, summarising, showing interest). Use a shape such as the one in Figure 10.3 with blank spaces for pairs to summarise their activity.

● Did you have more in common than you thought?
● What were the barriers when you spoke?
● How did you feel about sharing personal information?
● What can you learn from this when working with parents?

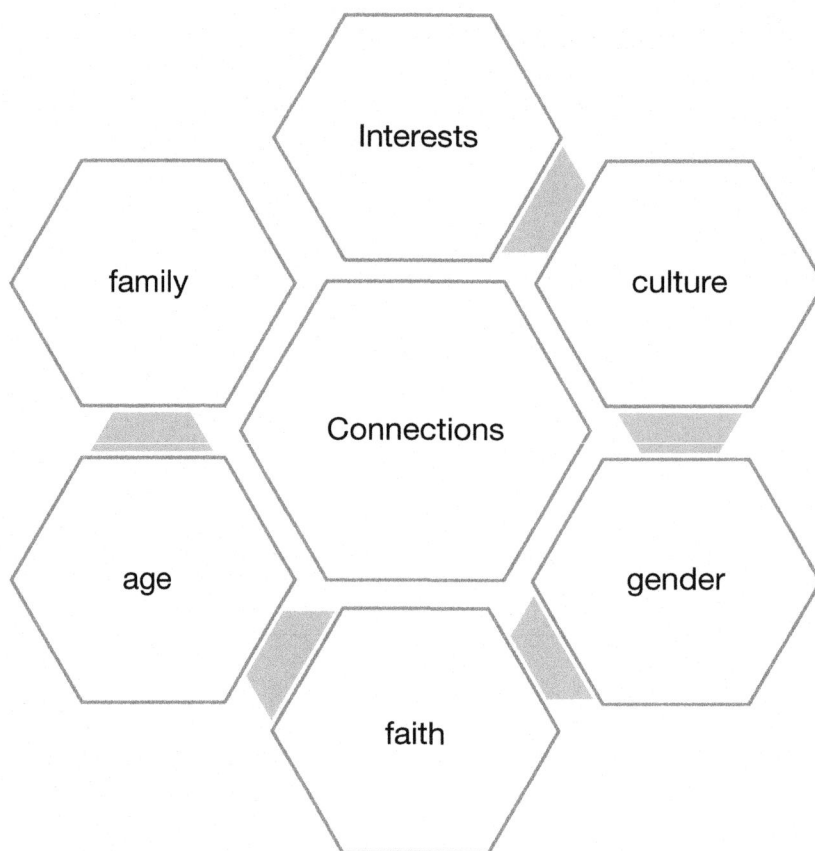

FIGURE 10.3 Finding connections with families

This activity can help you to reflect on ways that parents can feel that they belong in the setting – but it also makes you think about sharing information appropriately and maintaining boundaries. You might like to think about partnership working as one of a trio of possible working styles:

- befriending
- partnership
- expert.

In terms of working with parents, the **partnership model** is both seen by experts and embedded in policy and literature as being an appropriate model for use (CWDC, 2010; Davis *et al.*, 2002):

- Parents and helpers actively work together, involved and actively participating.
- Parents and helpers both influence decisions on what occurs.
- Parents and helpers value each other's knowledge, strengths and expertise and use these in complementary ways.
- Parents and helpers reach agreement on what they are trying to achieve and how.
- Parents and helpers resolve disagreement or conflict through careful negotiation, beginning from the parent's position.

- Parents and helpers show mutual respect and trust, involving interest, care and awareness of each other.
- Parents and helpers communicate clearly in ways that show openness and honesty. (CWDC, 2010).

Chapter review

By the end of this chapter, your team should be thinking more about the ways they communicate with parents and members of a wider family (Table 10.7). You will have had the opportunity to think about the communication methods that you use, and whether they are the most appropriate. You may have started thinking about the benefits of technology as a way of reaching parents who do not come regularly to the setting.

As with all relationships, change takes time and small changes can make a difference.

TABLE 10.7 Practice review

Chapter section	Fully engaged with strategies in place	Somewhat engaged	Further development needed
Whys and hows of communication			
EYFS: communication requirements			
Communicating			
Reading expressions			
Reflection on chapter			
What changes have you made?			
What needs further development?			

References

Brooker, L. (2010). Constructing the triangle of care: Power and professionalism in practitioner/parent relationships. *British Journal of Educational Studies, 58* (2), 181–196.

Children's Workforce Development Council (CWDC). (2010). *Families going forward learner resources.* Available: http://webarchive.nationalarchives.gov.uk/20111108140857/ http://shortbreakcarers.cwdcouncil.org.uk/families-going-forward-learner-resources

Davis, H., Day, C. & Bidmead, C. (2002). *Working in partnership with parents.* London: Pearson.

Department for Education(DfE) (2017). *Statutory framework for the early years foundation stage.* London: DfE.

Department for Education & Skills (DfES). (2007). Every *parent matters.* Nottingham: DfES.

Desforges, A. & Abouchaar, A. (2003). *The impact of parental involvement, parental support and family education on pupil achievement and adjustment: A literature review.* DfES Report No 433. DfES: Nottingham.

Epstein, J. (1995). *School/family/community partnerships: Caring for the children we share. The Phi Delta Kappa,* 76 (9), 81–96.

Goodall, J. & Vorhaus, J. (2010). *Review of best practice in parental engagement.* DfE RR 156. London: DfE.

Jack, R.E. (2013) Culture and facial expressions of emotion. *Visual Cognition, 21,* 1248–1286.

Killgore, W.D.S., Balkin, T.J., Yarnell, A.M., & Capaldi, V.F. (2017). Sleep deprivation impairs recognition of specific emotions. *Neurobiology of Sleep and Circadian Rhythms, 3,* 10–16.

Meehan, C. & Meehan, P.J. (2017). Trainee teachers' perceptions about parent partnerships: Are parents partners?. *Early Child Development and Care,* 1–14.

National College for Teaching and Leadership (NCTL) (2013). *Teachers' standards (early years).* Retrieved from: https://www.gov.uk/government/uploads/system/uploads/attachment_data/file/ 211646/Early_Years_Teachers__Standards.pdf

Office for Standards in Education (Ofsted) (2018). *Early years inspection handbook.* London: Ofsted.

Sylva, K., Melhuish, E., Sammons, P., Siraj-Blatchford, I., & Taggart, B. (2004). *The effective provision of pre-school education (EPPE) Project Final Report. A longitudinal evaluation (1997–2004).* London: DfES.

Wilson, T. (2016) *Working with parents, carers and families in the early yea*rs. Oxon: Routledge.

11 Working with families, special educational needs and disability

TABLE 11.1 Links to EY documentation

Teachers' Standards (Early Years), (NCTL, 2013)	Early years inspection handbook (Ofsted, updated 2018)	*Statutory framework for early years foundation stage (DfE, 2017)*
2.7 5.2 5.5 8.1 8.7	s. 151, p. 32	s. 1.6, p. 9 s. 1.7, p. 9

Parents whose children have a special educational need have a number of additional challenges that might result in lengthy calls on their time, financial costs – for example through visits to hospitals and specialists – and buying specialist equipment (Contact a Family, 2012), and increased stress levels. This is before managing the anxieties in relation to the condition itself.

In this chapter, you will find:

- activities to monitor staff experience in caring for children with disabilities;
- information about what the legal requirements of early years settings are;
- ways of communicating with parents sensitively in relation to concerns about a child;
- working with parents who are not ready to accept that their child needs extra support.

This chapter does not attempt to give detailed information about the development of EHC plans, or the interactions between local agencies in order to support a child with a disability. Rather its priority is to focus on the relationship with the parent and to ensure that harmony, support and cooperation are the dominant experiences in order to maximise progress, to give parents a sense of empowerment in that they are being listened to, and to offer them an expert ally when negotiating for their child's needs (Table 11.2).

TABLE 11.2 Practice reflection

Chapter section	Fully engaged with strategies in place	Somewhat engaged	Further development needed
Audit of staff experience			
Legal requirements			
Communicating sensitively with parents			
Assess, plan, do, review: a graduated approach			
When parents and practitioners disagree			
What strategies are currently in place?			
What needs further development?			

Audit of staff experience

Overnight reflection

Spend some time thinking about the range of factors that can inhibit children's learning and development. Are there areas where you are more experienced? Are you able to share the expertise you have with your colleagues at work (and they with you)?

Give the form in Table 11.3 to staff to complete and return to you, so you can build a database of staff experience and their level of confidence.

Use the list in Table 11.3 to gather information about your practitioners' expertise – there may be more than you think and sharing this can save time and develop confidence.

TABLE 11.3 Audit of staff experience

Name: Jenny Factor/condition	Experience of this condition (grade from 0–5, with 0 as no experience)
e.g. Autism spectrum	I have worked extensively with three children with ASD in a previous setting (4)
Asthma	3-year-old with mild asthma for short period (2)

Then compile the form in Table 11.4 by collating the information from staff. This may be helpful for the SENCO to maintain. Even if someone from your bank of expertise is unable to work directly with a family, they may be able to offer suggestions, contacts and encouragement.

TABLE 11.4 Staff skills information

Practitioner skills and experience	Practitioner A	Practitioner B	Practitioner C
Autism spectrum	Jenny has looked after three children on the autism spectrum and has good contacts for support groups		

Legal requirements of early years settings

Our understanding of special education needs has progressed significantly in the past 20 years and there is a much wider understanding of both the causes and the actions to be taken for a number of conditions, ranging from socio-emotional, cognitive to physical. In an early years setting, the initial signs that there may be developmental concerns are not easy to judge, because we know that:

> Children develop at their own rates, and in their own ways. The development statements and their order should not be taken as necessary steps for individual children. They should not be used as checklists. The age/stage bands overlap because these are not fixed age boundaries but suggest a typical range of development.
>
> (Early Education, 2012)

However, for the times when a problem may be emerging, being able to identify it rapidly can save time, costs and delays to development.

In addition to the legal requirements of working in partnership with parents (see Chapter 2), there is a UK legislative framework in relation to the support of children with Special Education Needs or Disability (SEND). This is the Special Educational Needs Code of Practice (DfE & DoH, 2015). Many of the underlying principles are included in the Equality Act 2010, which has a focus on discrimination and required reasonable adjustments (Citizen's Advice, 2018; HM Government, 2010).

Whilst the Equality Act is concerned with creating a society that is inclusive and takes into account a range of (adult's and children's) characteristics, the Children and Families Act has a different focus.

Children and Families Act 2014

The Children and Families Act 2014 (CFA) is not confined to disability. It is a wide-ranging act covering a range of areas relating to family life and support, including adoption and care proceedings, fostering and looked-after children, young carers, childcare, child welfare, statutory rights to maternal and parental leave and pay, and special educational needs. In terms of SEN, the Act has replaced the Statement of Needs with a new Education, Health and Care Plan (EHC).

Key points of the Education, Health and Care plan element of the Children and Families Act 2014 include the following:

- Education, Health and Care plan (EHC) replaces Statement of Special Education Needs and can be maintained up to 25 years.
- There is a duty for the local authority to publish a local offer, supplying information on local services.
- There is a duty to implement joint commissioning/integration of provision, considering and agreeing the educational, health and social needs of children and with involvement from parents and children in the decisions.
- SEN Support replacing School Action and School Action Plus.
- There is an expectation that the outcomes are aspirational.

We have already seen the requirements for working with families in the EYFS. You should note that it includes guidance on special educational needs.

Statutory Framework for the Early Years Foundation Stage (DfE, 2017)

Special educational needs

Section 3.67 (DfE, 2017, p. 31) states that:

> Providers must have arrangements in place to support children with SEN or disabilities. Maintained schools, maintained nursery schools and all providers who are funded by the local authority to deliver early education places must have regard to the Special Educational Needs Code of Practice.

Maintained schools and maintained nursery schools must identify a member of staff to act as Special Educational Needs Co-ordinator (SENCO) and other providers (in-group provision) are expected to identify a SENCO. Childminders are encouraged to identify a person to act as a SENCO and childminders who are registered with a childminder agency or who are part of a network may wish to share the role between them (DfE, 2017, p. 31).

In addition, a key document that specifies duties for organisations working with children and young people is:

> *The 2015 Special Education Needs Code of Practice* (Department for Education and Department of Health, 2015)

Within this document is reference to the principles underpinning the Code of Practice, for example, that:

> Local authorities **must have regard to:**
>
> - the views, wishes and feelings of the child or young person, and the child's parents;
> - the importance of the child or young person, and the child's parents, participating as fully as possible in decisions, and being provided with the information and support necessary to enable participation in those decisions;
> - the need to support the child or young person, and the child's parents, in order to facilitate the development of the child or young person and to help them achieve the best possible educational and other outcomes, preparing them effectively for adulthood.
>
> (DfE & DoH, 2015, p. 19)

This is therefore an inclusive and aspirational document, involving all those involved with the child and aiming for the best possible outcomes.

You will find a chapter relating to Early Years Providers on page 78 of the SEN Code of Practice, which gives detailed information about the requirements that providers must meet. In terms of working closely with parents, the message is clear throughout all documentation: **there is a requirement that you liaise with parents.** The Code of Practice notes that parents know their children best and that they should be listened to and understood (DfE & DoH, 2015, p. 79). Additionally, in section 5.7 (DfE & DoH, 2015, p. 80) it is stated that:

> Early years providers must provide information for parents on how they support children with SEN and disabilities, and should regularly review and evaluate the quality and breadth of the support they offer or can access for children with SEN or disabilities.

Longer activity: Leadership team including SENCO – reflection on supporting children with SEN and disabilities

Setting requirements:

- listening to parents;
- provide information on how the setting supports children with SEN and disabilities;
- thinking about what disabled children might require and what adjustments might be needed.

This is part of the anticipatory duty placed by the Equality Act (DoH & DfE, 2015, p. 80).

Look at these three bullet points and discuss a) how you are meeting these criteria and b) how they are evidenced. Add an action plan if there are elements that need further development.

The duties of the SENCO in the SEN Code of Practice 2015

The role of the SENCO involves:

- ensuring all practitioners in the setting understand their responsibilities to children with SEN and the setting's approach to identifying and meeting SEN;
- advising and supporting colleagues;
- ensuring parents are closely involved throughout and that their insights inform action taken by the setting; and
- liaising with professionals or agencies beyond the setting.

(DfE and DoH, 2015, para 5.54, p. 89)

You will see that one of the responsibilities of the SENCO is to ensure that parents are involved in decisions and have a voice in any actions taken. They are also responsible for leading and co-ordinating the graduated approach. You can find out more about what the role of the SENCO is here:

www.foundationyears.org.uk/files/2015/06/Section-6-Role-of-SENCO.pdf

Longer activity: Support from the SENCO and beyond

This is an opportunity for your team to work with the setting's SENCO in discussing aspects of multi-agency working. Organise a talk from the SENCO, focusing on these aspects and including discussion with the staff:

- the duties in the bullet points above;
- multi-agency working and the experiences that people have had;
- what the setting is doing well and how it can develop further.

Communicating sensitively with parents

You may want to talk to a parent who is new to the setting about their children's needs, or you might want to build a stronger relationship with an existing family in order that you can discuss some concerns you may have. A sensitive opening, leading from general topics to more specific ones, will help you to engage the parent more and show that you have a genuine interest. This is not always easy to implement in practice, in a busy setting, with little privacy and constant interruptions. Planning can help you get to know parents better.

Use this activity to plan and reflect on approaches to the first meeting.

CASE STUDY

John and Mary have twin boys, Jonah and Alfie, who are 18 months. They have approached your setting with a view to both the children coming to you. Jonah has a visual impairment that has recently been diagnosed. Alfie has some physical and motor developmental delays. Neither the key person nor the SENCO have met the family yet, but you know that the couple have an older set of twins who have just started school locally and that the parents are divorced.

———————————

In small groups, discuss how you will plan the first meeting with the family. Bear in mind that a family may have repeated conversations about their children's disability to a number of professionals for a number of years, so you may expect a range of responses from them.

The planning for the meeting will make a difference to whether parents see you as potential allies or practitioners who are taking up their time asking the same questions.

Whilst support should in theory be available for parents, it does not always come easily and 'the reality of obtaining support for children with SEND is that it can take longer than expected, and families can face additional challenges, long waits and disappointments' (Arnold, 2018, p. 35).

Using Table 11.5, make notes to plan for your discussions.

Table 11.5 Sensitive communication with parents: activity

Opening conversation to get to know the family
Listening to parents about their children's development
Identification and shared agreement of support for children
Finding out how the parents might be feeling
Sharing information of local support organisations
Any questions (at this point) to avoid asking

As you get to know families better and build strong relationships, you will identify the needs and aspirations of parents and children and help them to achieve them. The ongoing involvement of all parties can help with managing a diagnosis and sharing assessments is an important part of this. The SEN Code of Practice identifies a model to work with: assess, plan, do, review (DoH & DfE, 2015, p. 86) and stresses work in partnership with parents. Tenacity and perseverance are the keys to working with parents who do not appear to want to engage in a partnership, or who find that the reality of a diagnosis is a challenge to expectations and a blow to hopes. Maintain a positive approach and continually look for solutions to working together. In other words, be consistent in removing and overcoming barriers.

Assess, plan, do, review: a graduated approach

This is the expected process that takes place in settings, and is referred to in the Code of Practice. Parents and children should be involved in all of these steps in order to include their own views. You are likely to have documentation that records these statements and the actions that accompany them, as in Table 11.6.

While you consider the ways you work in partnership with parents, you may find it useful to visit some of the special needs parenting websites, for example, Special Needs Jungle (online, 2008–2018) which highlights the challenges and varied approaches that many parents experience. A look at a parent's website such as this helps to clarify the issues from a parent's point of view, including a fear of multi-agency working, a reluctance to be involved in a process that may appear daunting to one unfamiliar with the range of agencies, especially if English is not the family's first language. This is where a trusted practitioner could have a significant impact on a family by acting as a companion at meetings, a translator of complicated terminology and an emotional support. The use of empathy when working with parents whose children have disabilities can impart trust and a caring ethic for families when they are going through difficult and perhaps unexpected challenges in their children's lives.

Working with the parents who are not ready to accept that their child needs extra support

Notwithstanding the sensitive approach that you have been discussing, it is common to hear from practitioners that sometimes the parents they work with reject their suggestions that their child might have a learning need or need extra support. There are a number of reasons for this. For example, parents may feel:

- that they know their child better than anybody else and would know if something was wrong;
- reluctant to accept the reality of a potential disability and its implications;
- resistant to a message put across bluntly/tactlessly;
- unable to see problems because of subjective feelings about their own child;
- puzzled why no one else has mentioned it before;
- unable to manage the emotions that would follow from accepting that their child has a problem.

TABLE 11.6 Assess, plan, do, review: activity

Name of child

	Assess	Plan	Do	Review
Family feedback				
Practitioner feedback				
Wider professional involvement				
Next steps				

Longer activity: How might parents really be feeling?

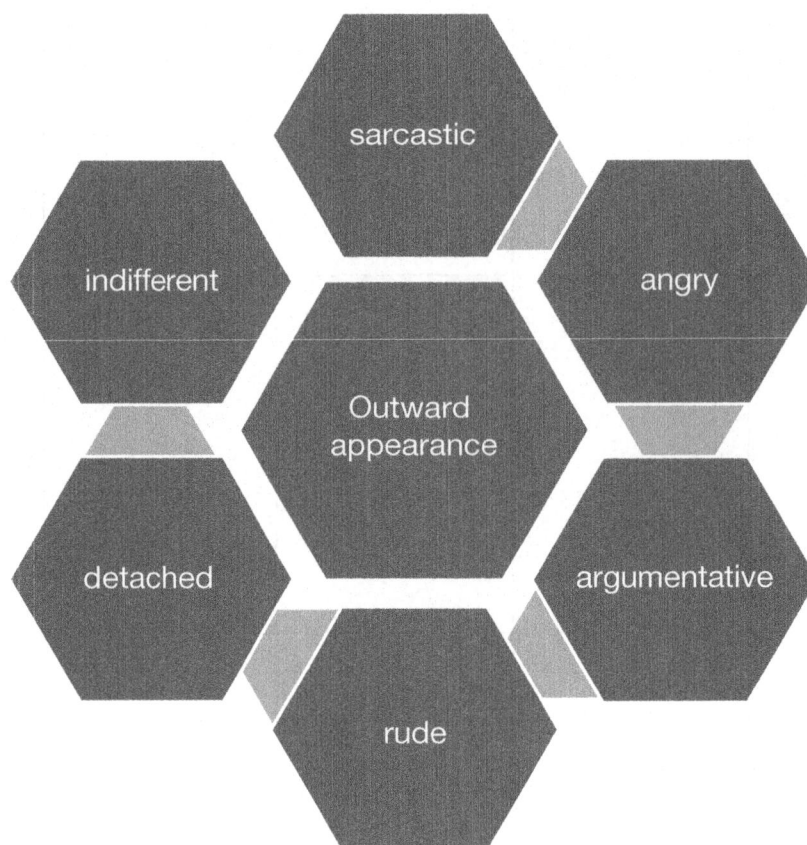

FIGURE 11.1 Outward appearances

How might parents be feeling or reacting when their responses are as shown in Figure 11.1?

You might feel frustrated yourself that someone 'blames' you for delivering the message of a child's developmental problem, or perhaps surprised that parents seem to be indifferent to your concerns.

Many of the emotions expressed at this time are not necessarily going to reflect how that parent actually feels. It is likely that the parent who appears to be indifferent either does not understand the situation or cannot reveal their true feelings. Even if the parent seems genuinely indifferent, this could be a cultural or language barrier, or it could be that something has happened in a previous experience that has resulted in that parent responding in this way.

In order to manage these events, discuss the range of ways that parents may present their ambivalent feelings with your colleagues, and then, consider how you would respond.

Short activity

In pairs, use the feelings on the diagram in Figure 11.1 as a prompt for possible scenarios; either carry out a role-play (one of you as parent, one of you as yourself) or share thoughts in small groups, considering possible responses from a parent.

1 Share with the group how this makes you feel, which will validate your feelings.
2 Next, respond professionally with what you could say to them, perhaps something like 'You say that Milly never does that when she is with you? Can you tell me a little more about what she does?'
3 Encourage the group to take turns and watch each other's role-play and offer ideas for useful strategies for maintaining your professionalism and also tips for defusing and situation and showing the parent that you are trying to understand them and support them.
4 Try this for all of the emotions that you have been discussing and write up the ideas that people have.
5 Use your listening skills (see page 44 in Chapter 3) to reflect your awareness of the parent's emotions and your desire to empathise.
6 Finally, role-play the real emotions that a parent may be suppressing when they snap at you angrily, or when they appear not to care. Practise a sensitive response to these (possibly strong) emotions.

Working with parents whose child has special educational needs or a disability is both challenging and rewarding, but there are some fundamental points to remember:

Key points

- assume that parents do want to be involved and identify barriers to their involvement;
- be kind and demonstrate empathy – it's part of your professional role to support parents;
- there is generally a reason why parents are unwilling to be involved and it is unlikely to be anything that you have done wrong – however, it may be possible for you to put right whatever has happened to make parents respond in this way.

In this chapter you have had the opportunity to consider the range of emotions that parents may experience when they are raising a child with a special educational need or disability. This experience has been likened to a bereavement, as parents adjust to the changing expectations of their child's life experiences. Your team's knowledge, experience and sensitivity can act as a support when working in this close partnership relationship (Table 11.7).

TABLE 11.7 Practice review

Chapter section	Fully engaged with strategies in place	Somewhat engaged	Further development needed
Audit of staff experience			
Legal requirements			
Communicating sensitively with parents			
Assess, plan, do review: a graduated approach			
When parents and practitioners disagree			
Reflection on chapter			
What changes have you made?			
What needs further development?			

Further reading

Council for Disabled Children: SEND Resources:
    https://councilfordisabledchildren.org.uk/help-resources/resources/focus-send
This is a useful guide to the SEN section of the Children and Families Act:
    https://councilfordisabledchildren.org.uk/sites/default/files/field/attachemnt/ChildrenAndFamilies
    ActBrief.pdf
Foundation Years: SEN Code of Practice:
    www.foundationyears.org.uk/files/2015/06/Section-6-Role-of-SENCO.pdf

References

Arnold, L. (2018). Working with parents: Principles of engagement. In R. Crutchley (ed.) *Special needs in the early years: Partnership and participation*. London: SAGE.

Children and Families Act. (2014). London: HMSO.

Citizen's Advice (2018). *Equality Act 2010 – discrimination and your rights*. Online: www.citizensadvice.org.uk/law-and-courts/discrimination/about-discrimination/equality-act-2010-discrimination-and-your-rights/

Contact a Family (2012). *Counting the costs 2012: The financial reality for families of disabled children across the UK*. London: Contact a Family. Available at: https://contact.org.uk/media/381221/counting_the_costs_2012_full_report.pdf

Department for Education (DfE) (2017). *Statutory framework for the early years foundation stage*. London: DfE.

Department for Education and Department of Health (2015). *Special educational needs and disability code of practice: 0 to 25 years. Statutory guidance for organisations which work with and support children and young people who have special educational needs or disabilities*. London: DfE.

Early Education. (2012). *Development matters*. Available at: www.early-education.org.uk

Equality Act (2010). London: HMSO.

HM Government (2010) Equality Act: guidance. London: HMSO. Available at: www.gov.uk/guidance/equality-act-2010-guidance#overview

National College for Teaching and Leadership (NCTL) (2013). *Teachers' standards (early years)*. Retrieved from: https://www.gov.uk/government/uploads/system/uploads/attachment_data/file/211646/Early_Years_Teachers__Standards.pdf

Office for Standards in Education (Ofsted) (2018). *Early years inspection handbook*. London: Ofsted.

12 | Concluding points

The only thing that remains is to consider how completing these activities has impacted the practice in your setting. You may have completed the beginning and end chapter reviews as you worked through some or all of the book. You may have engaged in a selection of activities, focusing on the importance of partnership work whereby parents and practitioners find it productive to work together, communicating and understanding the perspectives of all (Kambouri-Danos *et al.*, 2017) and discovering the benefits of collaboration in relation to the care and development of children.

This handbook has aimed to provide opportunities to collect evidence of your engagement with parents in a number of ways, and you may have invited parents to undertake surveys expressing your views. As practitioners and parents collaborate, new opportunities and information can be developed, such as (in Table 12.1):

TABLE 12.1 Reflecting on partnership work

• Planning open mornings and working with parents, e.g. observing children
• Better parent partnerships, with positive feedback from parents and practitioners
• Providing parents with more support
• Improving the quality of information sharing
• Supporting each other as a team
• Getting parents more involved in activities in the nursery so they can see the benefits of play
• Being more confident and using new ideas to build trust with parents to improve transitions
• Inviting parents to more everyday activities, not just events
• Using media to update a child's progress and communicate with parents
• Breaking barriers and building trust
• Taking both parents' and practitioners' perspectives into account
• Showing parents positive outcomes of activities e.g. through photos or observations
• Giving parents and practitioners the opportunity to explore and understand the ways that you can work together

It is helpful to remember that the purpose of working in partnership with parents is ultimately the maximising of positive outcomes for children: a shared desire, with shared support.

For your final chapter by chapter review, make notes on Table 12.2 to indicate whether anything has changed since you started thinking, reflecting and planning your partnership work.

If you feel that you have been making good progress with some of the ideas in Table 12.1, they could be developed into case studies for inclusion in setting publicity, evidence of partnerships for quality assurance or welcome packs for new parents so they can see your priorities.

Review on impact on practice

See Table 12.2 on the facing page.

It seems most appropriate to close this book with a quotation from an experienced practitioner who works with parents:

> Tenacity: keeping on, keeping on, keeping on. Slowly, slowly, drip, drip, drip. Sometimes there are an awful lot of barriers. My way of understanding is that part of the work with the child is the work with the parent. A parent may be very mistrusting, with cultural differences, language barriers, being fairly new to the country, so the more work you can do to build trust, that has an impact on a parent which has a knock on impact with the child and family that maybe people can be trusted. You've got to build that trust at a pace that is tolerable to parents.
>
> If you personally find something difficult on a subjective level, you have to try to leave your own feelings outside the door and try to understand the parent, and it might be quite difficult for you to understand if they are aggressive or offensive. But there's a much better chance of building bridges if you can leave your own feelings behind, which might help to understand their feelings. The barrier might be with you.
>
> (Wilson, 2016, p. 71)

TABLE 12.2 Chapter by chapter impact on practice

Chapter	Impact on practice	Date
Ch. 1	Making partnership with parents an outstanding quality in your setting	
Ch. 2	Policy, frameworks and the production of effective paperwork	
Ch. 3	Breaking down barriers	
Ch. 4	The beginning of your transformation: parental engagement in your setting	
Ch. 5	Supporting transitions – helping children and families adapt to change	
Ch. 6	Parental engagement in the baby room	
Ch. 7	Parental engagement in the toddler room	
Ch. 8	Parental engagement in the pre-school room	
Ch. 9	Creating a parent-friendly environment	
Ch. 10	Communication between parents and settings: sharing children's development and progress	
Ch. 11	Working with families, special educational needs and disability	
Ch. 12	Concluding points	

References

Kambouri-Danos, M., Liu, J., Pieridou, M. & Quinn, S.F (2017). Exploring the partnerships between parents and practitioners in the early years. *Early Years Educator, 19* (10), 26.
Wilson, T. (2016). *Working with parents, carers and families in the early years: The essential Guide.* Oxon: Routledge.

Index

Page numbers in *italics* refer to figures. Page numbers in **bold** refer to tables.